To the Church of God in the New River Presbytery,
with All the Saints Who Are in the Whole of West Virginia

CONTENTS

Preface to the Revised Edition vii
Preface to the First Edition ix
Introduction 1
The Builder 7
The Blueprint 15
Rough Framing 33
Finishing Work 47
Certificate of Occupancy 63
Site Cleanup 83
Moving In 91
Punch List 101
Final inspection 115
Endnotes 120

PREFACE TO THE REVISED EDITION

This edition revises and improves the first in several ways. Most obviously, I changed the title from *A Church You Can See: Building a Case for Church Membership*. The new, shorter title more clearly reveals the book's content and the construction motif.

Secondly, I have added discussion questions at the end of each chapter for one-on-one discipleship or study groups. I envision the book being used in Sunday Schools, new member classes, or church small groups, as well as by church leaders who are regularly discipling Christians one-on-one. I have purposefully included more questions than can be discussed in the space of a typical lesson, so leaders will need to pick which are most helpful for the moment. Ideally, the questions will inspire your own questions and paths for discussion.

Thirdly, I have corrected the text and improved the graphics and layout. The first edition was my first foray into book publishing under the ReformingWV Publications imprint. Since then I have grown as an editor and designer, so I thought I might go back and revisit this, my first self-published book. That being said, I am still not a professional editor or designer, which I expect will still show in places, with apologies.

Lastly, I removed the first edition's Presbyterian appendices in order to make the book more interdenominationally accessible. Thankfully, feedback on the first book was overwhelmingly positive, even by those who balked at my denomination-specific appendices. Hopefully, non-presbyterians may now be more willing to enfold this edition into regular church curricula. The original "presbyterian" version is still available under the old title for those who preferred it.

DEB
New Martinsville WV
November 1, 2019

PREFACE TO THE FIRST EDITION

Over the years, I have come to terms with the fact that I am not a professional scholar. So when I say that "this book has been written on a popular level," I am not trying to subtly inform you that I am the kind of person who—if I wanted to—could write things you wouldn't understand. Rather, it is because I did the best and most I can. Like most seminary-trained pastors, I am a theological and exegetical generalist. I hope I can be forgiven for whatever ways I have not fine-tuned my argument by scholars' standards. I am also not a contractor, so I also hope I can be forgiven for any ways I have failed to accurately apply the construction metaphor in this book. Professionals in both categories will immediately recognize any weaknesses, I am sure. But I wrote this for my State, my Presbytery, and my blue-collar brothers and sisters. As a proud, eighth-generation West Virginian, I simply want to communicate in a way that my beloved Appalachian family will receive and understand. In whatever ways it might still be over the heads of some, I hope that pastors will repackage it for their people. The topic is too important to keep out of the reach of our dear brothers and sisters in Christ.

I am grateful to the adult Sunday school class of Trinity Presbyterian Church in New Martinsville, West Virginia for attending the lessons that eventually resulted in this small book. They asked challenging questions, engaged in thoughtful discussion, and made original contributions. I am also grateful to God for experiences in previous churches that made me want to build a better case for church membership. And I am especially grateful to Fred Curry of Marmet, West Virginia, an elder and friend who alone and without reservation supported my conviction that churches should fence the table.

This book originated in very personal and pastoral circumstances. A church I once pastored rejected my efforts to fence the table in favor of allowing a non-member to participate in communion. The elders knew that this person had been unrepentantly "living in sin" for decades. But they argued that the church had no authority to tell someone they could or could not participate in communion: "The state of people's souls is nobody's business but their own. You have no right to judge others."

During that rejection, I realized two things: That my elders and congregation did not understand the importance and implications of church membership, and that I was not prepared to persuasively explain it to them. Both I and my congregation had a massive knowledge-gap. Unfortunately for that particular church, a persuasive biblical case for church membership was not within my reach, even as a seminary-educated minister. To aid my case, I researched other books on the subject, but they were more like handbooks: "Here is what church membership is like," instead of "Here is a strong theological and exegetical argument for church membership." In most cases, they failed to make a strong case that membership is anything more than a useful tool or practical necessity. In almost every case, they did not make a strong case for why communion must be tied to membership. So I failed to convince my congregation that membership in the visible church is crucial. When the elders finally demanded that I stop fencing the table, I resigned rather than violate my conscience. I had been unable to persuade them or the church.

Years later, I still encounter people inside and outside the church who place little value on membership. Many who are actively involved in a church could take it or leave it. I have even heard *pastors* question whether it is really necessary, and few can explain it as anything more than a tradition and a tool, only loosely related to real Christian living. Consequently, churches have diminished the value of the visible church and permitted the violation of what communion signifies. So I purposed to study, fill the gap, and set forth a persuasive, biblical case

Preface to the First Edition

for church membership. If I have not succeeded, I will be happy for others to create a stronger argument. The modern church desperately needs it.

There is much more to say about the church than what I have written—this is not an ecclesiology textbook. My goal has been singular and narrow: To persuade that membership is a biblical imperative. Christians cannot fully participate in the privileges and responsibilities of the church without confirming their union with Christ, committing themselves to the worship, work, government, and discipline of the church, and being received into the body by the church. Whatever else you may call it, this is church membership. It is crucial, because outside the visible church there is no ordinary possibility of salvation.

D.E.B.
New Martinsville, WV
August 10, 2017

1

INTRODUCTION

"I am a Christian, but I don't go to church. I don't believe in organized religion."

"I go to church every once in a while, like, once every few months. Definitely on Easter. And the Christmas Eve service. We always did that growing up, and it's still special to me."

"I go to church most Sundays, but I never joined. Never saw any need for it. All we do is sit, listen, and sing anyway. What's the point?"

"I joined the church because . . . well, I don't know why exactly. It's just what we always did every time our family moved to a new city. It's just what you do if you are a Christian."

"I definitely believe in church membership. Why? I don't know. It just makes sense. How else is a church going to keep track of everyone?"

"I want to take communion, but every time they have it, the preacher announces that only church members can partake. I guess I have to join a church."

Throughout my years of pastoral ministry, I have heard professing believers make all these statements (and more). I have observed some who never go to church and others who only go on occasional Sunday mornings. I have known others who attend church faithfully but never join. I have seen many who have joined but only because someone told them they should. I have known many with firm convictions about church membership, but who could not explain why if their souls depended on it.

Most who join churches don't ask too many questions. They do what most church members do: Visit around. Find a church they like. Attend for a while. Make sure it is the one for them. Join the church.

But I have known some to be more curious:

"Does the Bible really require membership? Can you show me chapter and verse? Isn't it a human convention? A long-standing tradition that at some point evolved into the norm? Is there evidence that the early church kept track of believers using applications, public testimonies, votes, and ledgers in church offices? If not, why do we have to?"

After thinking about it for a few months, some of them might still join the church:

"Oh well, I guess membership IS practical, even if it isn't biblically required. And I can't think of a clear scriptural reason not to. Maybe I should just go ahead and join."

But some will not:

"Church membership is not in the Bible. I want to attend regularly and participate, but I do not want to join. If the church has a problem with that, I will find one that doesn't push or practice membership."

What about you? Do any of these statements sound like something you might say? If you are a church member, could you persuade someone that church membership is biblical? Or would you get flustered after realizing that your strongest argument is "How else is a church supposed to keep track of everyone?" What if I were to tell you that a stronger case for church membership can indeed be found in Scripture?

The Construction Metaphor

In this book I will present what the Bible says about church membership using a construction metaphor: I will build a case for church membership like a builder builds a building. I will begin by telling you about the builder, and then I will move through the parts and stages of construction—the blueprint, the rough framing, the finishing work, the certificate of occupancy, and the punch list. When the building (or the case) is complete, I will invite you to move in.

Do not let my use of the *building* metaphor fool you into thinking that "church" is merely a building on a street corner. We all know it's more than that. The church is a kind of living, breathing organism that really does exist in this world. The building itself is not the church; the people who meet there are. My use of the construction metaphor is simply a way to organize my case for membership.

Overview

Construction will begin with the invisible and work its way toward the visible. The church is a spiritual organism, but it is not *just* a spiritual organism. It is not just a theological idea. It has both invisible and visible aspects. Just like buildings are material things extended in time and space, the church is visibly extended in time and space.

The visible church is fundamentally a church-you-can-see. We should be able to clearly identify its form and structure. It should be so easy to recognize that we can easily distinguish it from everything that is not the church. So in our case for membership, we will describe what makes the church visible to the naked eye. If we cannot see it, it is not there.

This book will make the case that the doors to the church-you-can-see are only found in particular churches. So if you choose to participate in the visible church, you have to walk through those doors. But it will also make the case that membership is more than a matter of choice, as though participation were optional. The privileges and responsibilities of the visible church are not optional for Christians. And if the doors to the visible church are only located in *particular* churches, then participating in a *particular church* is not optional. It is this participation that requires church membership.

Chapter Summary

With our construction metaphor in mind, we will first see how Jesus Christ is the *Builder* of the church. Then we will examine the *Blueprint* for our case by answering the question, "What is the pattern for the church?" The *Rough Framing* stage of construction will answer the question, "What shape does the church take?" In the *Finishing* stage of construction, a building is fitted with all the dried-in details, like plumbing and electricity. So at this stage we will answer the question, "What exactly is a finished church supposed to look like?" Once the building (or case) is ready for use, it receives a *Certificate of Occupancy*, which will answer the question, "What does participation in a church look like?" Next is the *Site Cleanup*, in which the entire case for membership will be tidied up and summarized. Once our building is ready for *Moving In*, we will address the question, "How do I go about actually joining a church?"

By the time we have built our way to this point in the metaphor, we will have constructed a case for a church that you can see, participate in, and join as a member. But the contractor is not yet finished. Most construction projects conclude with a *Punch List*—a list of problems that need to be resolved after the project is finished. So, I will address a question that will probably have occurred to some readers at some point in the book: "What about disagreements, differences, and denominations?" After that, we will conclude with a *Final Inspection*.

By the end of our construction project, we should see that God has given us specific privileges and responsibilities that can only be accomplished in the fellowship of a particular church. But before Christians can fully participate, churches must identify them and accept their commitment to these privileges and responsibilities. Call it what you will—this process of identification, commitment, reception, and documentation is church membership. And since the privileges and responsibilities of the church-you-can-see are not optional for Christians, neither is church membership.

Group Study and Discipleship: Introduction

Scripture Texts: Romans 12:4-5; 1 Cor. 6:15, 12:12

Discussion Questions:

1. What are your own convictions or opinions concerning church membership?

2. Do you believe that membership is biblically necessary? Or is it more of a tradition? Or is it best to think of it as a practical tool?

3. Have you met people who are opposed to church membership? How did they explain their position?

4. How have different churches in your experience approached the idea of membership? Are you aware of any churches that do not practice membership? What was good or bad about that? How did they keep track of people?

5. If you are a church member, why did you become one? What is your story? Have you had any unusual experiences in the development of your own convictions or opinions concerning membership?

6. What other metaphors could have been used to structure the book other than the construction metaphor?

7. What do you hope to get out of this class?

2

THE BUILDER

Matthew 16:13-19

> Now when Jesus came into the district of Caesarea Philippi, he asked his disciples, "Who do people say that the Son of Man is?" And they said, "Some say John the Baptist, others say Elijah, and others Jeremiah or one of the prophets." He said to them, "But who do you say that I am?" Simon Peter replied, "You are the Christ, the Son of the living God." And Jesus answered him, "Blessed are you, Simon Bar-Jonah! For flesh and blood has not revealed this to you, but my Father who is in heaven. And I tell you, you are Peter, and on this rock I will build my church, and the gates of hell shall not prevail against it. I will give you the keys of the kingdom of heaven, and whatever you bind on earth shall be bound in heaven, and whatever you loose on earth shall be loosed in heaven.

No construction project can begin without a builder, so our case for church membership must begin with Jesus. This famous passage from Matthew contains the first reference to the church in the New Testament. In it, Jesus Christ says that he himself will build his church.

Since the fall of mankind, the Son of the Living God has been assembling a people for himself out of all the tribes, tongues, and nations of the earth. Since the time Jesus lived and breathed on the earth, we have called this gathering of believers *the church,* a word which simply means "assembly."

Christ assembles his people together both *physically* and *spiritually.* Those who are assembled physically form the church-you-can-see. Those who are assembled spiritually form a church that you cannot see. It is invisible. Our case for church membership begins with this invisible, spiritual assembly. We can easily comprehend an assembly that we can see with our eyes. But what does it mean to say that Christ assembles people *spiritually*?

Union with Christ

Christ assembles people spiritually by uniting them together into himself. Thus, he builds his church through what we call *union with Christ.* To more fully understand this union, we will first consider a simple, man-made illustration, and then we will consider an illustration from Scripture that helps build our case for church membership.[1]

The Box Illustration

Imagine a box, and we believers are objects inside that box. Wherever that box goes, we go. Whatever is done to that box is done to us. If the box is carried to another room in the house, everything that is inside the box goes into that room along with the box. If we are not in that box, we do not go where the box goes or get what that box gets. *Union with Christ* is something like being placed inside that box.

Christ is righteous, so we get our righteousness by being placed in that box or "in Christ." Christ died in our place, and the reason his death counts for us is that God has placed us inside of Christ. We live with him because Christ lives (Galatians 2:20; Romans 6:1-14). We walk in newness of life because Christ was resurrected. Our physical bodies will be resurrected because Christ was resurrected (I Corinthians 15:22). We will be glorified because Christ was glorified (Romans 8:17, 29-30). We sit at the right hand of the Father with Christ even now, because we are in Christ (Ephesians 2:6). We will rule with Christ because Christ rules (2 Timothy 2:11-13). What happens to Christ happens to those who are in Christ.

If you study the New Testament, you will find *union with Christ* throughout. One of the best ways to locate it is to look for the simple phrase "in Christ." For example, read Ephesians and you will see the phrase immediately and repeatedly. When you see it, think of the box illustration. Remember that what happens to the box happens to what is in the box. What happens to Christ happens to us, because we are *in Christ*.

The Body Illustration

My box illustration is made-up. However, the Bible presents a much richer metaphor for our union with Christ—*the Body Illustration*. According to the Body Illustration, God wants us to think of the church in terms of a human body. It has members like arms and legs and hands and feet. Like all bodies, it has a head, which is in fact Jesus Christ himself (Colossians 1:18). The Body Illustration is found throughout Paul's epistles.[2] It reveals two truths that are important to our case for church membership: 1) There is only one body, and 2) that body is the church.

One Body

According to the Body Illustration, *all believers are united together in Christ to form a single body.* Just like all the parts of the human body form only one body, the many members of the body of Christ form only one body. This analogy is made very clear in the following passages:

1 Corinthians 12:12

> For just as the body is one and has many members, and all the members of the body, though many, are one body, so it is with Christ.

Ephesians 4:4-6

> There is one body and one Spirit—just as you were called to the one hope that belongs to your call—one Lord, one faith, one baptism, one God and Father of all, who is over all and through all and in all.

Romans 12:4-5

> For as in one body we have many members, and the members do not all have the same function, so we, though many, are one body in Christ, and individually members one of another.

One Church

The Body Illustration also shows that *the body of Christ is in fact the church*. This is clear from the following passages:

Ephesians 1:22-23

> And he put all things under his feet and gave him as head over all things to the church, which is his body, the fullness of him who fills all in all.

Ephesians 5:23

> For the husband is the head of the wife even as Christ is the head of the church, his body, and is himself its Savior.

Colossians 1:18-24

> And he is the head of the body, the church. . . . Now I rejoice in my sufferings for your sake, and in my flesh I am filling up what is lacking in Christ's afflictions for the sake of his body, that is, the church . . . .

When we combine these two truths, the Body Illustration shows that *all believers are united together into Christ to form one body, which is the church*. Therefore, to be in Christ is to be in the body. To be in the body is to be in the church.

No Dismembered Christians

The Bible never speaks of believers who are in Christ but who are not also in the body of Christ. Therefore, it knows nothing of Christians who are not in the church. No member of the human body—an arm, a leg, a foot—can live if separated from the body. Similarly, no believers can live outside the body of Christ. This means that those who are not in the body of Christ are not united with Christ. Since *union with Christ* is the only means of salvation, those who are not united with Christ are not saved. Since believers are united with Christ into his body, and since his body is the church, we can say what the church has said for centuries:

> "The visible church, which is also catholic or universal under the Gospel (not confined to one nation, as before under the law), consists of all those throughout the world that profess the true religion; and of their children: and is the kingdom of the Lord Jesus Christ, the house and family of God, out of which there is no ordinary possibility of salvation.[3]

Another way saying this is, "If you are in Christ, then you are in the church. If you are not in the church, then you are not in Christ." This challenging statement should help people to understand that the case for church membership is deadly serious. After all, "no ordinary possibility of salvation" is really intense. It definitely deserves more explanation. We will get to that, but for now, consider that ignoring, dismissing, or minimizing the importance of the church is really risky business for anyone who claims to be a Christian.

Site Inspection

In keeping with our construction metaphor, most of the following chapters will end with a job site inspection. Construction forepersons will frequently walk through the job site to check on progress, supervise employees, and look for safety issues. Our purpose will be to briefly summarize the main ideas of each chapter to see what progress we have made toward building our church membership case. These summaries will be in two parts. First is a propositional summary, which simply presents the logical steps in our case for church membership. Subsequent chapters will add a narrative summary, which will present the flow of my argument with a little more context and explanation. The site inspection will also provide a transition to the next stage of the case's construction.

In this chapter, we have learned that the Builder unites all Christians together into himself to form one body, which is the church. In other words, all Christians are members of the church. So, our case begins with the following simple premise:

If you are a Christian, then you are a member of the church.

You might be asking, "But *which* church are you talking about? Aren't there lots of different churches?" or even "What exactly do you mean by *church*?" It is true that there are lots of different churches, and the word can be used in different ways. What are the differences between these uses, and what do they have to do with church membership? The answer must be important, because "there is no ordinary possibility of salvation outside the church." So as we continue to build our case for church membership, we will first answer the question, "What do we mean by c*hurch*?"

Group Study and Discipleship: The Builder

Scripture: Matt. 16:13-19; Rom. 12:4-5; 1 Cor. 12:12; Eph.1:22-23; 4:4-6; 5:23; Col. 1:18-24

Discussion Questions:

1. Thinking through the construction metaphor, what does this chapter teach that earns it the title "The Builder?"
2. Christ said he would build his church. If Christ is in heaven, what role does he actively play in building his church today? What means does he use?
3. What is Union with Christ?
4. What is Paul's Body Illustration and how does it fit with the doctrine of Union with Christ?
5. The author made up his Box Illustration to illustrate Union with Christ. If you were explaining the concept to someone else, what illustration might you make up? Can you think of something better than the box illustration?
6. On p. 11, the text quotes the *Westminster Confession of Faith* (25:2). What other word-pictures (like "box" or "body") does this section of the confession use for the church? What do these add to your understanding of the church and our union with Christ? Are they biblical?
7. What are two truths (pp. 9-10) that can be gleaned from Paul's Body Illustration? How do you think the author will use these to build his case for church membership in the following chapters?
8. What do you think the *Confession* means when it says, "outside the church there is no ordinary possibility of salvation?"

9. The author said, "If you are in Christ, then you are in the church. If you are not in the church, then you are not in Christ." What might someone who disagrees say in reply? How would you respond to the person who disagrees?

10. The chapter concluded with the following summary-statement: *If you are a Christian, you are a member of the church.* Can you think of any way around this conclusion?

11. What are some different ways we use the word *church* in our everyday language?

12. Explain the difference between the visible and the invisible church.

13. Did you notice that the *Confession* was talking about the *visible* church instead of the *invisible* church? What is this distinction implying? How might this make some people uncomfortable?

14. Read note 3 in the endnotes about the reference to the *Westminster Confession of Faith*. Even though the *Confession* originated with Presbyterians, discuss whether the point still has value for other denominations. How would you change it to make it better fit your denomination, while still keeping the main idea?

3

THE BLUEPRINT

"I belong to the 'big-c' Church, but I do not belong to a 'little-c' church."

The word *church* has different uses. One church scholar says, "Sometimes it is used with respect to an architectural structure, a building. Frequently it is used to refer to a particular body of believers; we might, for example, speak of the First Methodist Church. At other times, it is used to refer to a denomination, a group set apart by some distinctive; for instance, the Presbyterian church or the Lutheran church."[4] Sometimes the word is used for all Christians or Christianity in general, without referring to any specific place or group of people. So when the Bible uses the word *church*, what does it mean?

We will use the blueprint of Scripture to answer that question. Construction always begins with blueprints that show the pattern for a project. A fundamental pattern found in Scripture is the distinction between the *visible* and the *invisible church*—the church that we can see and the church that we cannot see.

The Invisible Church

The invisible church is obviously the part of the church that we cannot see. It exists spiritually and is made up of the souls of all believers past and present. Jesus Christ has been populating this church since the beginning of time. By now, it no doubt comprises countless souls—like sand on the seashore or stars in the sky—although only God knows the exact number. The saints in heaven are a part of the invisible church, along with every true believer who is alive-and-well on the earth today (Heb. 12:23).

Scripture mentions the invisible church in many places. In Matthew 16:17-18, Christ himself builds the church, and nothing can ever destroy it. In Hebrews 12:23, the church is the assembly of the firstborn who are enrolled in heaven. In Colossians 1:18 and Ephesians 1:22-23, the church is Christ's body, and he is the head. In Ephesians 5:25-27, Christ gave his life to cleanse the church from sin and present it to himself perfect and without blemish. In Ephesians 3:3-10, and 1 Corinthians 12:12-13, the church comprises people from every tribe, tongue, nation, and class.

The Visible Church

On the other hand, the visible church is that part of the church that we can see with the naked eye. It contains only professing Christians who are still alive on planet earth. While all Christians past and present are members of the *invisible* church, only those who still have bodies are in the *visible* church. This means that when believers leave this world, they leave the visible church. The visible church only exists in the material realm—the here-and-now. However, it is both spiritual and material at the same time—it contains believers' physical bodies as well as their eternal souls. When they leave the visible church (i.e., when they die), they remain in the invisible church.

The Blueprint

The Bible does not recognize a category of living, breathing Christians who are not a part of the church-you-can-see. It presumes that if you still have a body (just like anyone reading this), you are part of the visible church. This creates a problem for body-having Christians who have little interest in the visible church. We will discuss that problem in greater detail in a moment. First we want to see that this visible church is actually taught in Scripture.

The Body Illustration (Again)

The Body Illustration is one of the easiest ways to locate the visible church in Scripture. Most references to the body of Christ pertain to the visible church. This makes sense. When we think of bodies, we think of something that can touch and be touched. This physicality is what makes the Body Illustration so useful for describing a church that is visible to the eye.

How can the body of Christ—the visible church—touch and be touched? How can it be seen by the eyes? Like the members of any human body work together (arms and hands, legs and feet), the members of visible churches work together. Only live human beings can participate in the privileges and responsibilities of the visible church. Most of these privileges and responsibilities are tangible—they require more than theories, ideas, or theological propositions. They require "boots on the ground." So when Scripture speaks of members of the body of Christ using gifts and abilities in the church, it always refers to the church-you-can-see.

The tangibility of the visible church is so important that I believe it is worthwhile to read the three most extensive *Body Illustration* passages in their entirety. None of what these passages are requiring can be accomplished by anyone who refuses to be a part of the visible church:

Romans 12:3-8

> For by the grace given to me I say to everyone among you not to think of himself more highly than he ought to think, but to think with sober judgment, each according to the measure of faith that God has assigned. For as in one body we have many members, and the members do not all have the same function, so we, though many, are one body in Christ, and individually members one of another. Having gifts that differ according to the grace given to us, let us use them: if prophecy, in proportion to our faith; if service, in our serving; the one who teaches, in his teaching; the one who exhorts, in his exhortation; the one who contributes, in generosity; the one who leads, with zeal; the one who does acts of mercy, with cheerfulness.

Ephesians 4:1-16

> I therefore, a prisoner for the Lord, urge you to walk in a manner worthy of the calling to which you have been called, with all humility and gentleness, with patience, bearing with one another in love, eager to maintain the unity of the Spirit in the bond of peace. There is one body and one Spirit—just as you were called to the one hope that belongs to your call—one Lord, one faith, one baptism, one God and Father of all, who is over all and through all and in all. But grace was given to each one of us according to the measure of Christ's gift. Therefore it says, "When he ascended on high he led a host of captives, and he gave gifts to men." (In saying, "He ascended," what does it mean but that he had also descended into the lower regions, the earth? He who descended is the one who also ascended far above all the heavens, that he might fill all things.) And he gave the apostles, the prophets, the evangelists, the shepherds and teachers, to equip the saints for the work of ministry, for building up the body of Christ, until we all attain to the unity of the faith and of the knowledge of the Son of God, to mature manhood, to the measure of the stature of the fullness of Christ, so that we may no longer be children, tossed to

and fro by the waves and carried about by every wind of doctrine, by human cunning, by craftiness in deceitful schemes. Rather, speaking the truth in love, we are to grow up in every way into him who is the head, into Christ, from whom the whole body, joined and held together by every joint with which it is equipped, when each part is working properly, makes the body grow so that it builds itself up in love.

1 Corinthians 12:12-31

For just as the body is one and has many members, and all the members of the body, though many, are one body, so it is with Christ. For in one Spirit we were all baptized into one body—Jews or Greeks, slaves or free—and all were made to drink of one Spirit. For the body does not consist of one member but of many. If the foot should say, "Because I am not a hand, I do not belong to the body," that would not make it any less a part of the body. And if the ear should say, "Because I am not an eye, I do not belong to the body," that would not make it any less a part of the body. If the whole body were an eye, where would be the sense of hearing? If the whole body were an ear, where would be the sense of smell? But as it is, God arranged the members in the body, each one of them, as he chose. If all were a single member, where would the body be? As it is, there are many parts, yet one body. The eye cannot say to the hand, "I have no need of you," nor again the head to the feet, "I have no need of you." On the contrary, the parts of the body that seem to be weaker are indispensable, and on those parts of the body that we think less honorable we bestow the greater honor, and our unpresentable parts are treated with greater modesty, which our more presentable parts do not require. But God has so composed the body, giving greater honor to the part that lacked it, that there may be no division in the body, but that the members may have the same care for one another. If one member suffers, all suffer together; if one member is honored, all rejoice together. Now you are the body of Christ and individually members of it. And God has appointed in the church first apostles, second prophets, third teachers, then miracles, then gifts of healing, helping, administrating, and various kinds of tongues. Are all apostles? Are all prophets? Are all teachers? Do all work miracles? Do all possess gifts of healing? Do all speak with tongues? Do all interpret? But earnestly desire the higher gifts.

Did you notice some common elements in each of these uses of the Body Illustration? Do you see the practical way Paul applies it? Real human beings are expected to use their gifts and abilities in service to one another. That is at least one way the body can touch and be touched. These passages are not talking about the church in theory, as if it existed only in the spiritual realm. It is talking about the church in practice—real, live Christians working together as one on this earth.

And speaking of working together as one, did you notice the emphasis on *unity* within this earthly body? All believers are to be unified in the body, which is the visible church. By definition, those who refuse to participate in the visible church cannot be unified in the body. They must ignore all that these passages demand regarding unity. We cannot be separated from the visible church and still be obedient to these portions of God's Word.

The Relationship of the Visible Church to the Invisible Church

Since the church exists in both invisible and visible forms, how do the two relate to each other? Figure 1 illustrates the answer.

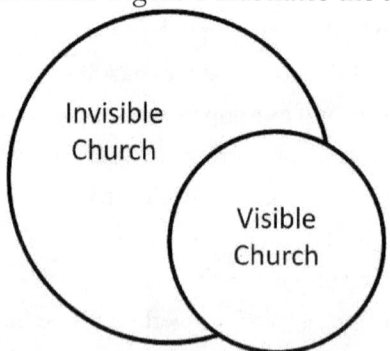

Figure 1. The Relationship of the Visible and Invisible Church

Note that the visible church overlaps the invisible church, but it is not entirely inside. Unfortunately, this is because the visible church comprises both true believers and false believers. The part that is outside the invisible church represents false believers. On the other hand, some *claim* to be Christians who never set foot in the visible church. They would theoretically be in the part of the invisible church that does not overlap with the visible. How can false believers be *in* the visible church and true believers on the *outside*?

False Believers Inside the Visible Church

False believers are people who claim to be Christians but are not true believers. On the basis of a false profession of faith, they are sometimes received into membership in the visible church. How is this possible?

The answer is that the visible church is finite or *limited*. Finite people cannot see the invisible soul (only God can see the heart), so they must rely on professions of faith and evidence of repentance to admit people to membership. Theoretically, only true believers should participate in the visible church, because only true believers are members of the *invisible* church. But finite people must trust those who profess faith in Christ, giving the benefit of the doubt unless they have obvious reasons not to. This may be gracious, but the downside is that sometimes non-Christians are welcomed into the visible church.

How can a non-believer profess Christ? There are two possible explanations: 1) either the non-Christian deceives others, or 2) the non-Christian is self-deceived. In the first case, we must acknowledge that people sometimes lie. They know in their hearts they are not born again, but for some reason they want to join a church anyway. In the second case, we must acknowledge that people are able to deceive themselves. They may think they are Christians when in fact they are not, and so they make a false profession of faith in order to join a church.

Regardless of how non-Christians enter the visible church, they are definitely here. The Bible notes this (I John 2:19; I Corinthians 11:19), and Jesus himself described false believers in his story about the farmer who sowed seed on different types of ground. Nothing came of one batch of seeds. Another batch was choked by weeds, thorns, and brambles. Another batch grew up strong and healthy. However, one of the batches initially looked like it was going to grow and bear fruit, but it eventually became clear that it was not:

Matthew 13:20-21

> As for what was sown on rocky ground, this is the one who hears the word and immediately receives it with joy, yet he has no root in himself, but endures for a while, and when tribulation or persecution arises on account of the word, immediately he falls away.

Jesus also warned about weeds that live among the wheat (Matthew 13:24-30) and wolves that dress in sheep's clothing (Matthew 7:15-23). There is little the church can do about non-Christians in the visible church unless and until they are revealed for who they really are. When they are revealed, church discipline becomes very important. I will say more on that topic later.

True Believers Outside the Visible Church

Then there is the opposite problem. Some who profess to be true believers do not participate in the visible church. Maybe they attend every once in a while, or maybe the never attend. Still they claim to be Christians. They may not believe the visible church is important, or they might not recognize the visible church when they see it. They may be good people by common Christian standards, doing good works and demonstrating Christian love. They might strive for justice and peace in this world in the name of Christ. They might pray and worship and study the Bible on their own. They may be obedient to Christ in many things, while at the same time ignoring or being ignorant of what God expects of all Christians with respect to the visible church. You might hear them say things like this:

> *"What do you mean I am not a part of the church? I spend a lot of time with Christians doing good things in my community. They are my church."*
>
> *"I belong to the 'big-c' Church, but I don't belong to a 'little-c' church. And I think that is good enough."*
>
> *"I am a Christian, but I do not believe in organized religion."*
>
> *"I cannot find a church that fits me, so I just worship and study on my own."*
>
> *"I got hurt badly in my last church, so I stopped going."*
>
> *"I have too many other things going on right now to fit church into the mix."*

No Ordinary Possibility of Salvation

What are we to think of self-proclaimed Christians who have little or nothing to do with the visible church? We will first admit that only God knows whether or not these people are truly born again. We will also admit that the church has historically allowed for the possibility that some people outside the visible church are indeed saved. The *Westminster Confession of Faith* says, "Out of [the visible church] there is no *ordinary* possibility of salvation."[5] The word *ordinary* grants the exception to the rule. It says that salvation normally brings people into the church, while acknowledging that, under extraordinary circumstances, some true believers may remain outside the visible church.

The existence of exceptions should not provide a sense of assurance and security for those who knowingly refuse to participate in the visible church. Unfortunately, we very easily wield exceptions to justify wrong behavior. We are often too quick to argue that "My circumstance is different!" If we are honest with ourselves, we will admit our own self-justifying tendencies. We have all rationalized wrong behavior at some time or another.

To show how easy it is to rationalize exceptions, consider this illustration: A video once made the rounds on social media. Ben Shapiro, a conservative, Jewish, pro-life advocate, was filmed presenting his pro-life position at a college. After his talk, he took questions from the audience. One defiant young lady took her turn at the microphone and asked, "What would you say to a woman who is pregnant because of rape or incest?" Knowing that less than 1% of all abortions occur in cases of rape or incest, Shapiro responded, "Okay, if I grant that abortion should be permitted under those particular circumstances, would you be willing to discuss preventing abortion in all other circumstances?" The young lady quickly replied that women should always have the choice to abort regardless of the circumstances: "It's her body. She should be able to do what she wants with it."

This scene quickly demonstrated that the young lady's exception was simply a rationalization for the position she truly wanted. In her heart, she believed the exception in one case should be the rule in all cases. Similarly, Christians outside the church should be quick to examine whether or not their "exceptional circumstances" are simply justifications for doing what they want instead of what God wants.

Lest there be any misunderstanding, let me state clearly that the Bible teaches that salvation is only and always by faith in Jesus Christ. Baptism never saves anyone. Neither does participating in communion or joining a church. We have already seen that non-Christians exist within the visible church. Presumably they have been baptized and regularly partake of communion. Obviously, being in the visible church does not guarantee salvation. So why has the church historically insisted that salvation and the visible church are ordinarily inseparable?

There are at least three reasons: The first is that the church is the divinely ordained steward of the Gospel through which God saves souls. The apostles were first commissioned by Christ to build his church by proclaiming the Gospel throughout the entire world. Repeatedly in Scripture they warned the church against adulterations of the Gospel. Alongside the Apostles, God gifted prophets, evangelists, and pastor/teachers for the purpose of keeping the church on the same page with regard to doctrine and practice (Ephesians 4:11-16). Today, the church sends out Gospel-preachers to every tribe, tongue, and nation. As the Gospel spreads, church elders are to be ordained in every location (Titus 1:5). They are to continue the divinely-ordained process of stewardship and instruction (Titus 1:9).

The second reason is that the church is in the business of "accrediting" claims to salvation. This is done through baptism, communion, and church discipline (how and why will be explained in the *Finishing Work* chapter). I know "accrediting" is an unusual word to describe what the church does. As a bi-vocational pastor who is also a college educator, I borrow it from the academic world. Simply put, accreditation is the process by which an agency certifies that a college is what it says it is and does what it says it does. Similarly, the church uses baptism, communion, and church discipline to certify that Christians are what they say they are and do what they say they do. Once "accredited," the church provides their ministry-home and assembles them regularly for worship and instruction according to the plan of God.

The third reason is that the Word of God teaches that Christians do not knowingly continue in sin. Those who do should not consider themselves Christians, and churches have no grounds to consider them

Christians. The First Epistle of John was written to inform people how they can know whether or not they have truly been born again. It presents many different applications of a very simple formula: All believers keep God's commandments. Those who do not keep God's commandments are not Christians—

1 John 2:3-6

> And by this we know that we have come to know him, if we keep his commandments. Whoever says "I know him" but does not keep his commandments is a liar, and the truth is not in him, but whoever keeps his word, in him truly the love of God is perfected. By this we may know that we are in him: whoever says he abides in him ought to walk in the same way in which he walked.

For many, this is a scary thought. It sounds so black and white. Doesn't every one sin? How can anyone ever have assurance of salvation? Indeed, everyone sins. First John 1:8 makes that clear: "If we say we have no sin, we deceive ourselves, and the truth is not in us." But John continues by reminding us that Jesus is the sinners' advocate and that God justly and faithfully forgives all who confess their sins. What John means is that the Christian's life is not characterized by unrepentant sin: "No one who abides in him keeps on sinning; no one who keeps on sinning has either seen him or known him (1 John 3:6). Those who are Christians live lives characterized by love for God and love for their brothers and sisters in Christ (I John 2:9-11; 3:10-18, 23; 4:7-8, 20-21; 5:1-3). Those who do not love their brothers and sisters in Christ are not themselves "in Christ." First John therefore raises two questions: 1) Do people who want little to do with the earthly assembly of their brothers and sisters have grounds to consider themselves Christian? And 2) do people whose lives are characterized by disobedience to God's expectations for the visible church have grounds to consider themselves Christian?

More than this, does the *church* have grounds to consider them Christian? Granting entrance into the communion of the church is a primary means by which the church certifies its confidence in people's profession of faith. Through admission to the sacraments (or ordinances), the church declares that it believes someone is truly a Christian.[6] On the other hand, "excommunication" is the means by which the church withdraws that confidence. What then is the church to think of all those who refuse to participate in the church's sacraments and submit to the church's discipline? At the least *the church* has no grounds to consider them Christians, no matter what they may believe about their own salvation.

Now back to the exceptions. What might be some legitimate, extraordinary examples of true believers outside the visible church? As it should be, it is hard to say with 100% confidence. The following spring to mind: What if you are the only believer in a large, third-world community? What if you are a believer in a country that has made it impossible to gather with other believers? What if you were taught incorrectly through no fault of your own? What if you move to a new area and can't find a good church? What if you are disabled and unable to attend church? What if you are a Christian in a family that forbids you or otherwise makes it difficult for you to be a part of a church? I am sure others can think of many other possibilities.

Regardless, I think that it is safe to say that, if it is in any way possible, true believers should participate in the visible church. At the least, those who have no obstacles other than their own disinterest probably misunderstand or ignore what the Bible teaches about the visible church. If they are ignoring what the Bible teaches, they are persistently rebelling against God. If they are persistently rebelling against God, then they have no grounds for claiming to be believers. The issue then is twofold: 1) Outside of obedient participation in the privileges and responsibilities of the visible church, do Christians normally have the right to an assurance of their salvation? And, 2) does the church have any obligation to recognize the salvation of those who claim to be Christians but refuse obedient participation in the privileges and responsibilities of the visible church?

"Churchless Christians"

Self-proclaimed Christians outside the visible church tend to fall into one or more of the following categories. These are general for simplicity's sake (extraordinary exceptions have already been granted). But most people in these categories would do well to consider that "out of [the visible church] there is no ordinary possibility of salvation."

Lone-wolf Christians

Lone-wolf Christians do not appear to have any commitment to the visible church. When questioned, they tend to justify themselves by rationalizing their lack of church attendance. They are often critical of organized religion and are sometimes convinced they know better than the people in the churches around them. They think of themselves as misfits or feel out of place at most churches.

Satellite Christians

Satellite Christians differ from Lone-wolf Christians in that they may not reject the visible church outright; they just never seem to settle down. They circle churches or congregations like satellites orbit the earth—a few Sundays at this church and a few at that one. They may value church attendance without recognizing the importance of making a commitment. Christians who have recently moved a great distance might seem like satellite Christians while they explore their options. However, they will eventually settle into a church—unless they misunderstand or ignore what the Bible teaches about the visible church.

Parachurch Christians

Parachurch Christians prefer to participate in Christian groups or organizations instead of a particular church. They might even believe that participating in parachurch ministries is the same as participating in the visible church (this is what I meant when I said earlier that they might not recognize the visible church when they see it). *Parachurch* refers to any Christian organization that operates *alongside* the church, like homeless shelters, soup kitchens, college or teen outreach organizations, missionary agencies, discipleship organizations, Christian colleges, Christian publishers, and many others. Parachurch organizations might be good and necessary, but they are not churches. Those who replace church with parachurch ministries either ignore or misunderstand what the Bible teaches about the visible church.

Disgruntled Christians

Disgruntled Christians have had experiences so bad that they refuse to go to any church. Of course, not all churches are worth attending, and not all Christians who leave churches because of bad experiences are disgruntled Christians. People can be seriously hurt by other Christians, and some churches need to be left in the dust. However, to leave the visible church entirely either ignores or misunderstands what the Bible teaches about visible church.

The-Bible-Doesn't-Teach-Membership Christians

Some Christians do not believe the Bible teaches church membership. Perhaps they were brought up in church traditions that do not practice church membership (there are several). Or perhaps they have "studied" the issue and have privately interpreted that church membership is not necessary. In the case of the former—their church tradition probably still had some practical means for identifying its participants and providing or restricting access to its privileges and responsibilities. Call it church membership or not; those means still accomplished the same goals. If their church tradition did not in fact have some means of identifying the church and providing or restricting access to the church's privileges and responsibilities, then it either misunderstood or ignored what the Bible teaches concerning the visible church.

Incidentally, if you fall into this category and you are now attending a church that does in fact practice church membership, consider this question: whatever your past practice and whatever your present conviction, do the church leaders whom you now expect to care for your soul require membership in order to participate in the full privileges and responsibilities of the church? If the answer is "yes," then how will you obey Hebrews 13:17 without becoming a member of the church? Look it up. This will come up again later.

Site Inspection

If you are a Christian, then you are a member of the church.

If you are a member of the invisible church, then you ought to be a member of the visible church.

Part of the church can be seen, and part of it cannot. All believers belong to the part of the church that we cannot see, but the Bible presumes that those who are alive-and-well on planet earth will obediently participate in the part of the church that we can see. Those who do not participate in the visible church are either disobeying or ignoring what the Bible teaches about the church we can see. This leads us to the question of the next chapter: "If the church is in fact something that we can see, what shape does it take?"

Group Study and Discipleship: The Blueprint

Scripture: Rom. 12:3-8; Eph. 4:1-16; 1 Cor. 12:12-31

Discussion Questions:

1. Thinking through the construction metaphor, what's in this chapter that earns it the title "The Blueprint?"
2. What are some different ways we use the word *church* in our everyday language?
3. With reference to this particular chapter, what is the fundamental pattern—the blueprint—for the church that we find in Scripture (p. 15)?
4. Explain the difference between the visible and the invisible church.
5. The chapter quotes Romans 12:3-8; Ephesians 4:1-16; and 1 Corinthians 12:12-31. What do we find in all three of these passages that imply that the visible church is a very real thing in this world and not just a spiritual thing that we cannot see (p. 20)?
6. Explain how it is possible for false believers to be inside the visible church?
7. What is a biblical perspective on self-proclaimed Christians who want little or nothing to do with the visible church?
8. Why has the church historically insisted that salvation and the visible church are ordinarily inseparable (p. 25)?
9. The *Westminster Confession of Faith* says that "Out of [the visible church] there is no *ordinary* possibility of salvation." What does the word *ordinary* mean in this sentence? What are some legitimate exceptions that might be included in the meaning of the word *ordinary*?

10. Do you think human nature is more likely to abuse exceptions or use them properly? Which do you think is more likely to be true for most Christians who want nothing to do with church: that they have good reasons or are illegitimately rationalizing their lack of participation?

11. From your own experience, can you give specific examples (without naming names) of poor reasons to not participate in the body of Christ?

12. The book lists several categories for self-proclaimed Christians outside the visible church (pp. 28-30). Can you think of any categories that are not listed? Or can you name some interesting examples from your experience (without naming names) and then figure out which category they belong in?

13. As a general rule, can you think of any reason why someone who claims to be a Christian should not ordinarily be a part of the visible church?

14. Do you agree or disagree with the chapter's summary statement: *If you are a member of the invisible church, then you ought to be a member of the visible church?*

4

ROUGH FRAMING

Our task in this chapter is equivalent to the rough work of a construction project. We will take what began as a blueprint and start framing it up for all to see. As the frame goes up, the structure will begin to take shape. Building-frames are real things made of wood and metal. They have dimensions that can be measured with a tape measure. They are held together by nails and screws. When they are "in the dry," they are complete enough to keep us from getting wet when it rains.

Unlike the spiritual nature of the invisible church, the visible church also has real weight and dimension in this world. Returning once again to the Body Illustration, the human body has weight and dimension. Human bodies, after all, are physical things; spirits are not. Like building frames, the church has a very real form or shape in this world. What shape does it take?

As we have said, Scripture presents the visible church as a body with many members. It would be handy if the Apostle Paul used the word *member* to refer directly to church *membership,* because that would make our case easier. But he doesn't. He simply uses it to refer to members of a human body, like arms, legs, feet, and so on. Jesus did the same thing in Matthew 5:29-30, as did the Apostle James in James 3:5-6. It is a familiar expression, which is what makes the Body Illustration so relatable. Consider these examples from Scripture:

Romans 12:4-5

> For as in one body we have many members, and the members do not all have the same function, so we, though many, are one body in Christ, and individually members one of another.

1 Corinthians 6:15

> Do you not know that your bodies are members of Christ?

1 Corinthians 12:12

> For just as the body is one and has many members, and all the members of the body, though many, are one body, so it is with Christ.

The Shape of the Church

It should be obvious that the members in these passages are real, live, human-beings in real, live churches. These members are what make the church visible. But the primary point of the body illustration is always that these real, live human beings are connected to form a whole. The visible church may be *many* but it is also *one*. There is always a larger structure to the body— each part is the church, but all of it is also the church. Thus, *the church is a polymerized plurality of particular churches.*

The Visible Church is Particular

If I scoop up a handful of sand at the beach and examine it carefully (with my reading glasses on) I can make out individual grains of sand. Each of these would be *particular* grains. When we refer to *particular* churches we mean individual local churches, just like the one that meets in your home town in that building with the steeple and stained-glass windows. The Scriptures identify many particular churches. They usually met in private homes and were each considered churches in their own right:

Romans 16:5

> Greet also the church in [Prisca and Aquila's] house.

1 Corinthians 16:19

> Aquila and Prisca, together with the church in their house, send you hearty greetings in the Lord.

Colossians 4:15

> Give my greetings to the brothers at Laodicea, and to Nympha and the church in her house.

Philemon 1:1-2

> Paul, a prisoner for Christ Jesus, and Timothy our brother, to Philemon our beloved fellow worker and Apphia our sister and Archippus our fellow soldier, and the church in your house.

The Visible Church is Plural

A particular church is an individual church, but there were hundreds of individual churches spread throughout the Roman Empire. This means that the visible church contains a plurality of particular churches. This is obvious, of course, but for good measure, here is the evidence from Scripture:

Romans 16:16

> Greet one another with a holy kiss. All the churches of Christ greet you.

1 Corinthians 7:17

> This is my rule in all the churches.

1 Corinthians 11:16

> If anyone is inclined to be contentious, we have no such practice, nor do the churches of God.

1 Corinthians 16:1

> Now concerning the collection for the saints: as I directed the churches of Galatia, so you also are to do.

1 Corinthians 16:19

> The churches of Asia send you greetings.

2 Corinthians 8:1

> We want you to know, brothers, about the grace of God that has been given among the churches of Macedonia.

Galatians 1:22

> And I was still unknown in person to the churches of Judea that are in Christ.

The Visible Church is Polymerized

Here is where I may risk losing you in the details, but I have my reasons for being so particular (pun intended). Notice that when writers refer to a plurality of churches, they sometimes group them together by regions, territories, or cities. As they do, they sometimes address the entire group as a single church. Paul wrote each of his city-based letters to groups of churches in those cities, yet he addresses them to the church in each city as a whole. We do not know how many individual churches were in each city, but Ephesians was written to the churches that met in the city of Ephesus, Romans to the churches in Rome, Philippians to Philippi, Colossians to Colosse, and Thessalonians to Thessalonica. Galatians was written to churches in many different cities throughout a large region of the Roman Empire (Asia Minor). Though each city could have contained many particular congregations, Paul at times addressed them as one church:

1 Corinthians 1:2

> To the church of God that is in Corinth. . . .

2 Corinthians 1:1

> To the church of God that is at Corinth, with all the saints who are in the whole of Achaia. . . .

1 Thessalonians 1:1

> To the church of the Thessalonians in God the Father and the Lord Jesus Christ. . . .

2 Thessalonians 1:1

> To the church of the Thessalonians in God our Father and the Lord Jesus Christ. . . .

We see the same practice in Revelation, where Jesus told John to write directly to all the churches that met in seven different cities throughout Asia: "Write what you see in a book and send it to the seven churches, to Ephesus and to Smyrna and to Pergamum and to Thyatira and to Sardis and to Philadelphia and to Laodicea" (Revelation 1:11). Each of the seven cities may have contained several particular churches meeting in different homes. Yet all these churches are still addressed as *the* church (singular) of that city.

What the evidence tells us is that it is proper to call each individual congregation a church, and it is also proper to call a group of individual churches the church. This would be true no matter how we grouped the churches. Each would be the church and all would be the church. The church is one and many. We can visualize this with a diagram (Figure 2):

Figure 2. Each is the Church and all are the Church

I belabor this point because I have encountered churches that are so passionate about their independence that they deny the existence of the visible church beyond local congregations. To them, a proper church exists only as an independent, sovereign, local congregation. Scripture is clear that this is wrong. Our evidence says that the visible church can be considered as one and as many at the same time. All of it is the church, and each part is the church. The visible church is therefore a polymerized plurality of particular churches.

The Oxford Dictionary defines a *polymer* as "a substance that has a molecular structure consisting chiefly or entirely of a large number of similar units bonded together." How did I come to use such a strange word—*polymerized*—to describe the church? Excellent question.

I first taught this material to my adult Sunday School class. I already had two *P* words—particular and plural—that were perfect for their part of the job, and I desperately wanted a third to communicate the way the entire visible church is made up of all the particular churches throughout the world. You know how preachers are—always looking for alliteration. I asked the class to think on it for a week and come back the following Sunday with any suggestions. The next week, a retired science teacher brilliantly suggested the word *polymerized,* which, strange though it may sound in this context, perfectly summarizes the way the entire visible church is made up of a vast plurality of particular churches throughout the world. So in this case, the word *polymerized* means that the entire visible church is made up of a large number of similar units—particular churches—repeated over and over again and bonded together in Christ. Spiritually, they are connected to one another to form one church.

A Connected Church

Ideally, if all these churches are connected spiritually—which they are—then their visible aspects should also be structurally connected as much as is practically possible. That is what a visible church would do, and that is the example we find in Scripture.

Consider again the letter of Revelation addressed to the seven churches. We do not know how many, but suppose there were three house churches in each city. Why would the letters not have been addressed to 21 churches instead of to only seven? The answer is that when John (and Jesus) wrote to the church within a certain city, they expected the letter to be distributed to all churches within that city even though they still referred to all these churches collectively as the *church.* This implies that the visible church was structurally connected. A letter addressed to the church in a region would need to be reliably communicated to all its particular churches. Such transmission would require some structural connection among the churches: at least a roster of congregations and open lines of communication. Similarly, when Paul addressed an epistle "To the church of God that is at Corinth, with all the saints who are in the whole of Achaia" he reveals the same expectation. What's more, we know these rosters and lines of communication were used to manage the visible church. We find this illustrated in Acts 15, where a council of elders (under the leadership of Jesus' brother James) met in Jerusalem and provided authoritative leadership to many different churches throughout the rapidly growing church. The application of this biblical church structure is that particular churches should be connected together in some form or fashion to form a larger visible church.

Figure 3. *The Spectrum of Church Connections*

Most particular churches recognize that they are part of something much bigger, a spiritual whole. Most churches also recognize that they should try to represent this wholeness in the way the church is structured. Churches may differ on exactly how to connect themselves to one another, but throughout history they have tried many different ways to unite congregations together. Once again, there have always been exceptions—separatists of sorts who think every church should stay out of every other church's business (often labeling themselves as *independent*). But among those who do recognize the need for unity in the church, methods for unifying fall out on the spectrum of prelacy, presbyterianism, and partnerships (Figure 3).[7] More alliteration!

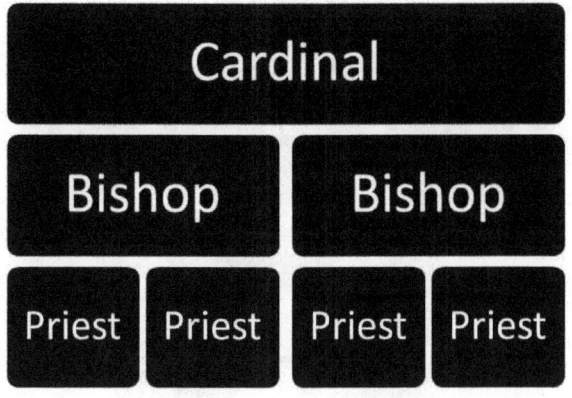

Figure 4. Prelacy

Prelacy

On one end of the spectrum lies *prelacy* (Figure 4).[8] Prelacy organizes the church by means of hierarchies of church leaders—a sort of top-down command structure with popes and cardinals, bishops and priests all possessing different levels of authority. Because each answers to a superior, they together create a type of unity, much like a military might move and act in unison within the command structures of generals, colonels, majors, captains, lieutenants, sergeants and privates. The chief examples of these are the Roman Catholic Church, Orthodox churches, and Anglican or Episcopalian churches.

Partnerships

On the other end of the spectrum are those who do not believe that any church should be under the control of any other church, but they still recognize that there is ultimately only one church. They might attempt to manifest that unity through voluntary *partnerships* (Figure 5).

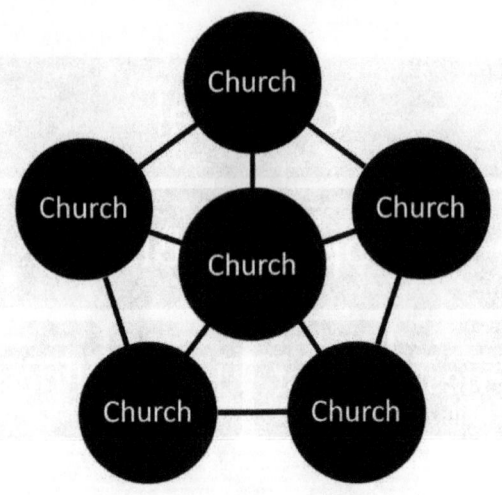

Figure 5. Partnerships

In the partnership model, congregations partner with other congregations of like mind to form groups that can demonstrate unity and work together toward common goals. Their arrangement still allows each particular church to maintain a high degree of self-control. Among these are various kinds of baptists and other congregationalists.

Presbyterianism

In between these extremes are a variety of other ways to relate each church to a larger group of churches. They usually try to balance a blend of top-down authority and congregational independence.

For instance, my own denomination is *presbyterian* (Figure 6). Each congregation chooses elders to form an elder-board called a *session*. These elders join together with elders from other churches in a region to form a presbytery. Presbyteries meet together to form a general assembly. The presbyteries' and general assembly's authority among particular congregations is powerful, but presbyterianism still reserves much power and authority on local levels. For instance, all decisions about daily operations, use of property, and kinds of ministries are up to each church. Also, the elders who comprise the larger bodies are still freely elected by each congregation.

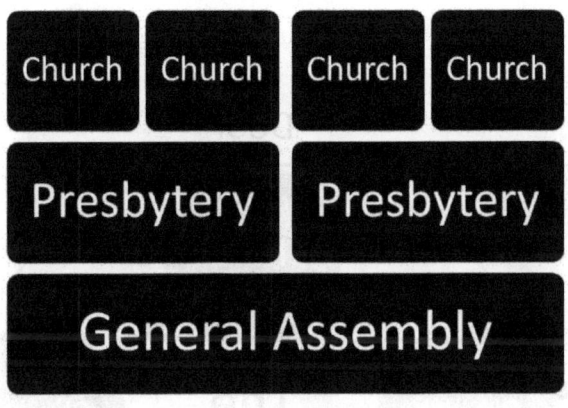

Figure 6. Presbyterianism

No single method of organizing the church has been completely successful at creating a unified church. This is due to our finiteness and sinfulness (which you can read more about in *The Punch List* chapter). Nevertheless, the fact that the church is not yet visibly united into a single whole has not stopped churches from joining together with other churches to form larger groups of the church in obedience to Scripture's demand for unity.

The Doors to the Church

In this chapter, I have demonstrated that individual churches form the larger visible church. How does this build our case for church membership? By leading us to this conclusion: No Christian can claim to be a part of the visible church without participating in the local church. However the church is connected, no portion of the visible church is constructed of any material other than particular churches. Particular churches are the building blocks of the visible church. This means that there is no entrance into the visible church that is not also a door to a particular church (Figure 7).

In other words, one cannot be a part of the visible church without being a participant in the local church.

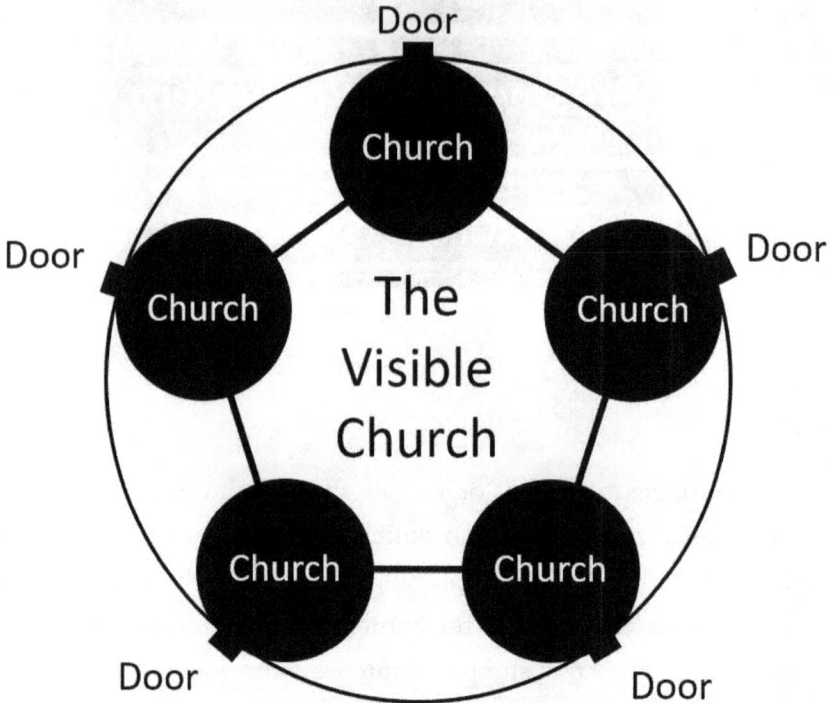

Figure 7. *The Doors to the Particular Church*

Site Inspection

If you are a Christian, then you are a member of the church.

If you are a member of the invisible church, then you ought to be a member of the visible church.

Rough Framing

You cannot be a member of the visible church without participating in a particular church.

Part of the church can be seen, and part of it cannot. All believers belong to the part of the church that we cannot see, but the Bible presumes that those who are alive-and-well on planet earth will obediently participate in the part of the church that we can see. Those who do not participate in the visible church are either ignoring or are unaware of what the Bible teaches about the church we can see.

The part of the church that we can see, the visible church, comprises a polymerized plurality of particular churches. These churches can be connected together in different ways, but there is no avoiding the fact that apart from participation in a particular church Christians cannot be obedient participants in the visible church. This raises the question, "How can we know a particular church when we see one?" We must be able to identify particular churches if we are going to obediently participate in the visible church.

Group Study and Discipleship: Rough Framing

Scripture: Rom. 16:5, 16; 2 Cor. 1:1

Discussion Questions:

1. Thinking through the construction metaphor, what's in this chapter that earns it the title "Rough Framing?"

2. What does it mean to say that the church is particular? That it is plural? That it is polymerized?

3. Which of the above three is most debatable? Have you ever encountered someone who believes the church only exists in the form of local, independent congregations? Tell about your experience. How would you counter them?

4. Using a different letter of the alphabet, can you alliterate three words that convey the same meanings as the above three? [e.g., "L"--Local, Lots-and-lots, Linked.]

5. Presbyterianism is listed in between the extremes of prelacy and partnerships. Can you describe other ways churches connect (besides presbyterianism) that also lie between prelacy and partnerships? Bonus points for alliteration!

6. The book asserts that the only doors to the visible church are located in particular churches. Can you think of exceptions?

7. One of the implications of this chapter is that *you cannot be a member of the visible church without participating in a particular church*. Agree or disagree? Can you think of any exceptions?

8. Looking ahead, what are the marks of a particular church? List some things that distinguish the church from any other Christian organization.

5

FINISHING WORK

After buildings are framed, construction workers begin the finishing stage of construction: wiring, plumbing, insulation, sheetrock, flooring, cabinetry, etc. At this stage, a walk-through makes very clear what kind of structure is being constructed. Is it a house? Is it a store? Is it a church building? By the time the finishing stage is complete, inspectors should have a good sense of what everything is going to look like when it is finished.

In keeping with our building metaphor, we will now add to our case the scriptural principles that show what a church should look like when it is finished. We will call these the *marks of the visible church*. They will help us to distinguish the visible church from everything that is not a church. In short, I will make the case that if a "church" does not have elders, then it is not a church. If it does not meet together for worship, instruction, and the sacraments, then it is not a church. If it does not practice church discipline, then it is not a church.

Historically, the marks of the visible church have been listed as 1) the true preaching of the Word, 2) the right administration of the sacraments, 3) the faithful exercise of discipline. I firmly agree with these historical marks, but I have reorganized, reframed, expanded, and subsumed them in a way that I believe better serves a modern case for church membership. Anyone concerned with their apparent absence in what follows can see them fleshed out in the details of this chapter and the next.[9]

The Visible Church Has Elders

1 Timothy 3 calls the role of elder an *office*, which means that it was an official, ordained position within the church. It is one of only two continuing offices in the visible church.[10] Without the office of elder a church cannot properly be called a church.

The history of elders stretches back into the Old Testament. Israel lived under elder leadership for millennia. Originally, older men governed their tribes and families. Many of these were appointed to a more official capacity in Israel when God commanded Moses to ordain them as elders and officers (Numbers 11). From that time on, the role of elder has continued as an office in Jewish communities.

In the New Testament, the elder office was also divinely ordained for the leadership of the visible church. Only men who met strict criteria qualified for the office. As Christianity spread, appointing elders was one of the necessary steps for putting churches in proper order (Titus 1:5). The New Testament usually speaks of the elders in each city and church in the plural, which is why churches should ordinarily have a plurality of elders. In Acts 14:23, Paul and Barnabas "appointed elders for them in every church." Today, some churches have only a single pastor (and maybe assistant or associate pastors), while their board of deacons serves in an elder-like capacity. Regardless of what they are called, they act as elders.

According to 1 Timothy 5:17, some of the elders in each church were paid to preach and teach. Today our custom is to call paid preachers *pastors* to distinguish them from elders who are not employed by the church. However, the words for *pastor, elder,* and *overseer* (aka *bishop*) originally referred to the same office regardless of who did the preaching (cf. Acts 20:17; Philippians 1:1; 1 Timothy 3:1-7; Titus 1:5-7). In many churches today, the words are still used interchangeably, and all the elders have equal authority (or parity). Regardless, a church is not a church without elders, pastors, or overseers, whether or not they go by those names.

Acts portrays elders as having a place of ruling-authority within the church (15:2-6, 22-23; 20:17; 21:18). Hebrews 13:17 commands believers to obey and submit to their elders. Elder authority extends to doctrinal and moral issues, as well as conflicts between believers within the church (Acts 20:28; I Peter 5:1-3; I Corinthians 5:9-6:7). Of course, elders do not have the right to abuse their authority (I Peter 5:3), but the fact remains that a person who is not under the care of elders is not participating in the visible church.

The Visible Church Meets Together

The English word *church* translates the Greek word for a*ssembly* or *congregation*. In the Old Testament, the word *church* meant "the assembly or congregation of the Israelites, especially when gathered before the Lord for religious purposes."[11] This meaning carries over into the New Testament. The word for *church* was used specifically for its *assembly* connotation. Whatever else the church does, it assembles; it gathers; it meets together, because the church is never only one person.

The word is used for both the invisible and the visible church. As we have learned, the invisible church is spiritually assembled together into Christ through our union with Christ. But the *visible* church assembles physical bodies together in specific locations for specific purposes. Romans 16:5 and Philemon 1:2 show two examples of the visible church physically gathered together.

What exactly does the visible church meet together to do? Can we be more specific about this gathering activity? Based upon the scriptural evidence, I believe we can.

The Visible Church Assembles for Worship and Instruction

Just like the assembly of the Israelites gathered together for worship, the church in the New Testament does the same. We could look at many passages, but First Corinthians 14 provides several examples in one place. Paul gives instructions for proper behavior in church worship services. Several times he uses the word *church* in a way that can only refer to people assembled together for worship and instruction: "in church," "in the churches," and "the whole church comes together" (19, 23, 28, 34-35). He even says that unbelievers might sometimes gather with them (16, 23-24). He shows they were gathered for worship by referencing praying, thanksgiving, singing, and worship (14-16, 25-26). And he shows that they were gathered for edification and instruction by stressing how important it was to benefit others through instruction, prophesying, and interpreting (3-12, 19, 26-28). Paul concludes by telling them that worship, edification, and instruction in the gathered church "should be done decently and in order" (40).

The fact that the church gathers together for worship and instruction dovetails with the already-established fact that the visible church must have preaching and teaching elders. Instruction within the gathered church was so important that God ordained the office of elder specifically for that purpose (1 Corinthians 12:28-29; Ephesians 4:11-16). Qualified elders had to be "able to teach" (I Timothy 3:2) and were expected to "hold firm to the trustworthy word as taught, so that he may be able to give instruction in sound doctrine and also to rebuke those who contradict it" (Titus 1:9). Acts 6 portrays early church elders as having little time to do anything other than preaching and praying.

The sort of preaching and teaching described in these passages was accomplished primarily in gathered settings, and they were not optional for the early church. Neither are they optional for today's church. The author of Hebrews even warns against failing to gather together:

Hebrews 10:24-25

> And let us consider how to stir up one another to love and good works, not neglecting to meet together, as is the habit of some, but encouraging one another, and all the more as you see the Day drawing near.

Therefore a person who does not gather with other believers for worship, edification, and instruction is not participating in the visible church.

The Visible Church Assembles to Participate in the Sacraments

Christ ordained two sacraments to be celebrated in the church until he returns: baptism and communion. Some prefer to call them *ordinances* instead. Christ initiated baptism through the Great Commission, and he initiated communion at the Last Supper.

Baptism

Just as regeneration and union with Christ join people to the invisible church, baptism joins people to the visible church. Baptism is a fitting picture of both regeneration and union with Christ. Washing with water represents the cleansing work of the Holy Spirit (Ezekiel 36:25-32; Ephesians 5:26; Titus 3:5-6), and baptism so closely signifies the idea of union that the word actually means *union with Christ* in Romans 6:1-5 and Colossians 2:11-12. Of course, baptism has no power of itself to change hearts and unite people to Christ. But the sign and what it signifies are so closely tied together in Scripture that some people have wrongly concluded that it does.[12] Since baptism is the initiatory rite that joins people to the visible church, most denominations only practice baptism under the authority of ordained elders in the company of the gathered church.

Communion

First Corinthians 10:16-17 gives us two reasons we have come to call the Lord's Supper *communion*. First, it signifies our union and communion with Christ. In the English Standard Version, the Greek word for *communion* is translated *participation* in verse 16:

> The cup of blessing that we bless, is it not a participation in the blood of Christ? The bread that we break, is it not a participation in the body of Christ?

Secondly, it signifies our communion with the other believers with whom we are united in the body of Christ, the visible church (17):

> Because there is one bread, we who are many are one body, for we all partake of the one bread.

For these two reasons, obedient churches ordinarily practice communion only in the company of the gathered church. Paul's instructions concerning communion in 1 Corinthians 11:17-34 show this to be true no less than five times:

> But in the following instructions I do not commend you, because (1) *when you come together* it is not for the better but for the worse. For, in the first place, (2) *when you come together* as a church, I hear that there are divisions among you. And I believe it in part.... (3) *When you come together*, it is not the Lord's supper that you eat.... So then, my brothers, (4) *when you come together* to eat, wait for one another—if anyone is hungry, let him eat at home—so that (5) *when you come together* it will not be for judgment (numbering and emphasis added).

When we look at everything 1 Corinthians 10 and 11 says about communion, we see that communion is only intended for those who are united with Christ, united with the body of Christ, and pursuing unity within the body of Christ. This leads elders to *fence the table,* a practice by which they formally explain who may and may not participate. Fencing the table plays an important role in my case for church membership, so I will explain it in greater detail in the next chapter.

For now though, take note that the visible church meets together when celebrating communion precisely because of what communion means. Celebrating communion apart from the company of the visible church violates what it stands for. Any person or organization that practices communion outside the structure of the visible church (*a polymerized plurality of particular churches*) is not participating in the visible church. Those who do not participate in the visible church should not partake of communion.

The Visible Church Identifies Christians

When the visible church identifies Christians it distinguishes between those who can fully participate in the privileges and responsibilities of the church and those who cannot. Paul called those who could not *outsiders* or *strangers*. We have already seen in 1 Corinthians 14 that Paul expected *outsiders* to occasionally visit church meetings. Even though they assembled with the Christians, they were still called *outsiders*. These were people who had not been identified as believers or received into the number of the church through baptism. The biblical language of *outsider* makes no sense apart from this distinction.

In 1 Corinthians 5 and 6, Paul makes this distinction even more clear. The context is that some believers were suing one another in secular courts. Once again he refers to *outsiders* in contrast to those inside the church (5:12). He specifically states that some people have "standing in the church" and some do not (6:4). He refers to those who do have standing in the church as saints and brothers (6:1-2, 5-8) and those who do not as the unrighteous who "will not inherit the kingdom of God" (6:9).

Such a distinction implies that the early church identified Christians. I have encountered many people who are appalled at the idea that a church would dare "judge someone's spiritual condition." It is common in western society (and especially in my Appalachian circles—M*ontani Semper Liberi,* anyone?) to believe one's spiritual condition is nobody's business but one's own. Unfortunately for those who hold tightly to that belief, this flies in the face of the testimony of Scripture. Distinguishing between those inside and outside the church is only possible when the church exercises its right and responsibility before God to distinguish between Christians and non-Christians. This is accomplished by receiving people *into* the visible of church and expelling people *from* the visible church, neither of which is possible if the church has no right to judge anyone's spiritual condition. The church distinguishes Christians from outsiders through two means: baptism and church discipline.

Baptism

Though baptism saves no one, Christ ordained it to be the means by which people are admitted into the visible church.[13] It serves as an external sign of the spiritual work that only God can perform. What makes baptism a distinguishing activity is that it is administered only to those whom the church has determined meet the criteria for admission to the visible church.[14] Those who are baptized into the church form the group Paul refers to as having "standing in the church."

Church Discipline

The second activity through which the church distinguishes between Christians and non-Christians is church discipline. Receiving people into the church is not the hard part. Churches usually have no problem with evaluating testimonies of salvation and baptism when receiving people into the visible church. Baptisms and memberships are usually grand occasions, complete with potluck meals and cakes. But the church should recognize that every time it does this it is exercising its right and responsibility to distinguish between Christians and non-Christians. The rub comes when churches must move in the opposite direction—from inside to outside the church. If the church can determine that someone is qualified to be numbered among the believers, it stands to reason that the church can and should determine when someone is disqualified from being numbered.

As we have already seen, the visible church unfortunately contains both believers and unbelievers. The church cannot tell the difference until the unbelievers reveal themselves. Paul mentions them in 1 Corinthians 11:18-19:

> For, in the first place, when you come together as a church, I hear that there are divisions among you. And I believe it in part, for there must be factions among you in order that those who are genuine among you may be recognized.

John also mentions them in 1 John 2:19:

> They went out from us, but they were not of us; for if they had been of us, they would have continued with us. But they went out, that it might become plain that they all are not of us.

Once unbelievers reveal themselves—if they cannot be encouraged to true faith and repentance—they should be expelled from the church. The process of expelling people from the visible church is called *excommunication*. Those who have been "ex-*commune*-icated" have been removed from the same communion signified by the Lord's Supper. By removing people from the communion of the visible church, the church is expressing its judgment that the person does not have communion with Christ, or is not united with Christ. In other words, excommunication occurs when so-called believers are discovered to be unbelievers.

It is true that the visible church cannot see the soul. Only God can do that. But God has given the church the authority and responsibility, based upon what he has revealed in his Word and what it observes of its members, to excommunicate those in whose profession of faith it has lost confidence. We can demonstrate this from Scripture. Christ gives the church the authority and responsibility to exercise *church discipline* in Matthew 18:15-20:

> If your brother sins against you, go and tell him his fault, between you and him alone. If he listens to you, you have gained your brother. But if he does not listen, take one or two others along with you, that every charge may be established by the evidence of two or three witnesses. If he refuses to listen to them, tell it to the church. And if he refuses to listen even to the church, let him be to you as a Gentile and a tax collector. Truly, I say to you, whatever you bind on earth shall be bound in heaven, and whatever you loose on earth shall be loosed in heaven. Again I say to you, if two of you agree on earth about anything they ask, it will be done for them by my Father in heaven. For where two or three are gathered in my name, there am I among them.

When Christ says to regard someone "as a Gentile and tax collector," he was using language that his hearers understood to mean "outsider."

Church discipline is usually carried out under the leadership of the church elders, because they have been given the primary responsibility of shepherding the flock of God (1 Peter 5:2) and watching for the souls under their care (Hebrews 13:17). Because they are shepherding souls, the goal of church discipline is never excommunication, but rather restoration. This is why Jesus prescribed multiple steps. Rather than kicking unbelievers out, he wants us to gain brothers in the process.

However, sometimes sinners are unrepentant. Everyone sins, but not everyone sins unrepentantly. According to Scripture, only unbelievers do that (read through Hebrews and 1 John). According to Jesus, church leaders must confront unrepentant sin, dealing with it privately when possible and publicly when necessary.

When church leaders are commissioned upon threat of judgment to watch out for souls (Hebrews 13:17), they do not have the luxury of letting blatant and unrepentant sins continue. To do so would be to allow deep spiritual damage both to the church and to the person who is in sin. Anything that risks the judgment and damnation of the soul is by its very definition the responsibility of those who are ordained by God to care for souls. Elders cannot turn their heads and hope such problems disappear.

The price of losing a soul is too great to ignore unrepentant sin, both for the soul that is lost, and for the church leader that must give an account to God for the souls under his care. When church leaders must exercise this kind of authority, they do not do it with glee, or because they want to lord their authority over people, or because they like conflict. No one who does that should be a church leader. Rather, they exercise their disciplinary authority in the hope of full repentance and restoration.

Paul gives multiple examples of various stages of church discipline in several passages:

2 Corinthians 2:5-8

> Now if anyone has caused pain, he has caused it not to me, but in some measure—not to put it too severely—to all of you. For such a one, this punishment by the majority is enough, so you should

rather turn to forgive and comfort him, or he may be overwhelmed by excessive sorrow. So I beg you to reaffirm your love for him.

2 Thessalonians 3:6, 14-15

> Now we command you, brothers, in the name of our Lord Jesus Christ, that you keep away from any brother who is walking in idleness and not in accord with the tradition that you received from us. . . . If anyone does not obey what we say in this letter, take note of that person, and have nothing to do with him, that he may be ashamed. Do not regard him as an enemy, but warn him as a brother.

1 Corinthians 5:4-5, 11-13

> When you are assembled in the name of the Lord Jesus and my spirit is present, with the power of our Lord Jesus, [5] you are to deliver this man to Satan for the destruction of the flesh, so that his spirit may be saved in the day of the Lord. . . . But now I am writing to you not to associate with anyone who bears the name of brother if he is guilty of sexual immorality or greed, or is an idolater, reviler, drunkard, or swindler—not even to eat with such a one. For what have I to do with judging outsiders? Is it not those inside the church whom you are to judge? God judges those outside. "Purge the evil person from among you."

1 Timothy 1:18-20

> This charge I entrust to you, Timothy, my child, in accordance with the prophecies previously made about you, that by them you may wage the good warfare, [19] holding faith and a good conscience. By rejecting this, some have made shipwreck of their faith, [20] among whom are Hymenaeus and Alexander, whom I have handed over to Satan that they may learn not to blaspheme.

These passages and others (e.g. Galatians 6:1; Ephesians 5:11; Titus 3:10) present a range of responses to sin in the church. Some present great hope for restoration. Others present the severe fact of excommunication. This range reveals that this most difficult step should never done in haste, or with hatefulness and prejudice, but with sincere concern for the state of the soul and deep hope that the sinner might truly repent and return to Christ and the church.

Throughout church history, churches have done everything from admonishing sinners privately or publicly, suspending them from the Lord's Supper for a season, and—when worse comes to worse—excommunicating them from the church. Whether through baptism or church discipline, churches that do not distinguish between Christians and non-Christians are not doing what the visible church is expected to do.

Site Inspection

If you are a Christian, then you are a member of the church.

If you are a member of the invisible church, then you ought to be a member of the visible church.

You cannot be a member of the visible church without participating in a particular church.

Part of the church can be seen, and part of it cannot. All believers belong to the part of the church that we cannot see, but the Bible presumes that those who are alive-and-well on planet earth will obediently participate in the part of the church that we can see. Those who do not participate in the visible church are either disobeying or are unaware of what the Bible teaches about the church we can see.

The part of the church that we can see, the visible church, comprises a polymerized plurality of particular churches. These churches can be connected together in different ways, but there is no avoiding the fact that apart from participation in a particular church, Christians cannot be obedient participants in the visible church.

In keeping with our building metaphor, we have added to our case principles that give us a sense of what a particular church should look like. Historically, these principles have been called *the marks of the visible church*. We have learned that the visible church has elders, it meets together for worship, instruction, and the sacraments, and it identifies Christians. Wherever these marks are found, so is the church. This means that if a "church" does not have officers, then it is not a particular church. If it does not meet together for worship, instruction, and the sacraments, then it is not a particular church. If it does not practice church discipline, then it is not a particular church. If what you are participating in is not a particular church, then you cannot be an obedient participant in the visible church.

If it is not answered already, our next chapter will respond to the next logical question: Once a particular church has been identified, isn't it enough to just attend? Must a believer really go through the process of becoming a member?

Group Study and Discipleship: Finishing Work

Scripture: Titus 1:5; Heb. 10:24-25; 1 Cor. 5:1-6:11

Discussion Questions:

1. Thinking through the construction metaphor, what's in this chapter that earns it the title "Finishing Work?"

2. Should a parachurch Christian organization be considered "the visible Church?" Why or why not?

3. What are the marks of a particular church? List some things that distinguish a church from any other Christian organization.

4. Compare the author's marks of the visible church with the historic marks of the church listed on page 47. How are the historic marks subsumed or included in the author's marks? Is anything included in the author's marks that are not also included in the historic marks? Should the historic marks be revised?

5. Do you agree with the author's assertion that "an organization that does not have elders is not the visible church?" If not, why not?

6. Do you agree with the author's assertion that "an organization that does not meet together for worship, instruction, and the sacraments is not the visible church?" If not, why not?

7. Do you agree with the author's assertion that "an organization that does not practice church discipline is not the visible church?" If not, why not?

8. Why is baptism required for membership? Can baptism be separated or divorced from the process of membership? In

other words, should someone be baptized who has no plans to become a member of a church? If so, why?

9. For Presbyterians: Presbyterians baptize the infant children of believers, marking their place in the visible church. Why are these children considered a part of the visible church even though they have not yet made a profession of faith?

10. Why has baptism traditionally been performed by ordained elders and not by laypersons? Are these reasons strong or weak? What are the implications for baptism's association with membership if laypersons can also baptize people?

11. Do you believe that excommunication is biblical? Do you agree that it is in effect a withdrawal of confidence that the disciplinee is truly converted (or a true believer)? Do you believe this is going too far? Does the church have the right to declare that it does not believe someone to be converted?

12. What do you think it means to "hand someone over to Satan" (I Timothy 1:18-20)?

13. Have you observed church discipline done poorly? What went wrong?

14. Have you observed church discipline done well? What went right?

15. Have you observed church discipline that resulted in the restoration of the person under discipline? Can you give examples if appropriate?

16. Looking ahead, what do you believe are the privileges and responsibilities of those who participate in the visible church?

6

CERTIFICATE OF OCCUPANCY

The next stage in building our case for church membership is to issue the *Certificate of Occupancy*. Our building has been planned, framed, and finished. A certificate of occupancy certifies it is ready for use. Accordingly, we will now look at what this "use" looks like in terms of the visible church. We will see that God expects all believers to participate in specific privileges and responsibilities. These include pursuing unity, applying God-given gifts, receiving instruction, participating in the sacraments, and submitting to the government and discipline of the church. Because these cannot be completely fulfilled outside the context and care of particular churches, the process of church membership is necessary for all believers.

Christians Pursue Unity

The unity of the body of Christ is not an abstract idea. Scripture speaks of it as a visible reality. If nothing else, Paul's repeated reliance upon the Body Illustration is aimed at unifying believers within particular churches. Once again, examine the following verses:

1 Corinthians 12:24-27

> But God has so composed the body, giving greater honor to the part that lacked it, that there may be no division in the body, but that the members may have the same care for one another. If one member suffers, all suffer together; if one member is honored, all rejoice together. Now you are the body of Christ and individually members of it.

Ephesians 4:1-4

> I therefore, a prisoner for the Lord, urge you to walk in a manner worthy of the calling to which you have been called, with all humility and gentleness, with patience, bearing with one another in love, eager to maintain the unity of the Spirit in the bond of peace. There is one body and one Spirit—just as you were called to the one hope that belongs to your call.

Romans 12:3-5

> For by the grace given to me I say to everyone among you not to think of himself more highly than he ought to think, but to think with sober judgment, each according to the measure of faith that God has assigned. For as in one body we have many members, and the members do not all have the same function, so we, though many, are one body in Christ, and individually members one of another.

This unity is practical—a real person-to-person unity. It cannot be achieved by those who believe they have no obligation to consistently assemble with a particular group of believers. Christians who fail to unite themselves with particular churches either willfully or ignorantly disobey the will of God. If willfully disobedient, neither they nor other believers can have confidence in their claim to be Christian, because the unrepentant cannot lay claim to being Christian. They fit better into John's category of those who leave the church because they are not of the church.

Some may say that the biblical obligation to pursue unity does not require membership—after all, they may have attended the same church for years without being members. However, one can reasonably question the commitment to unity of any regular attender who refuses the commitment that church membership represents. Obedient Christians pursue unity with other believers, and this suggests that church membership is biblical.

Christians Use Their God-given Gifts in Service to One Another

Our reoccurring Body Illustration allows us to take the case for church membership a step further. The form that this unity must take is not mere church attendance, but active participation—using God-given gifts in service to other believers within particular churches. Paul brings the metaphor to bear upon the disunity that sprung out of the early church's diversity. He says every believer is different, but God himself is responsible for that diversity. Not only has he brought people together from diverse backgrounds (1 Corinthians 12:13), but he has gifted them with a variety of spiritual gifts and responsibilities (Romans 12:3, 6; 1 Corinthians 12:7, 11; Ephesians 4:7; cf. 1 Peter 4:10). Just like the human body, members function in the visible church in different but essential ways:

1 Corinthians 12:14-20

> For the body does not consist of one member but of many. If the foot should say, "Because I am not a hand, I do not belong to the body," that would not make it any less a part of the body. And if the ear should say, "Because I am not an eye, I do not belong to the body," that would not make it any less a part of the body. If the whole body were an eye, where would be the sense of hearing? If the whole body were an ear, where would be the sense of smell? But as it is, God arranged the members in the body, each one of them, as he chose. If all were a single member, where would the body be? As it is, there are many parts, yet one body.

Instead of dividing the church, God expects diverse gifts and responsibilities to unify the church. They are "for the common good" (1 Corinthians 12:7), and "for the building up of the body of Christ, until we all attain to the unity of the faith and of the knowledge of the Son of God" (Ephesians 4:12-13). So Peter says that Christians are to "employ [gifts] in serving one another. . . . so that in all things God may be glorified through Jesus Christ, to whom belongs the glory and dominion forever and ever" (1 Peter 4:10-11).

The unity that Paul's metaphor calls for is only possible when Christians use their gifts in service to one another in the context of the body of Christ, the visible church. God calls for something more than mere church attendance. He calls for Christians to use their gifts in service to other believers in particular churches. Since elders are responsible for equipping people for this service (Ephesians 4:11-12), most churches will expect those who desire to jump deeply into church ministry to demonstrate submission, accountability, and commitment to the church and its leadership. This demonstration is nothing less than what most churches call church membership.

Christians Receive Instruction

We have already demonstrated in the *Finishing Work* chapter that churches gather together to worship and receive instruction. The preaching and teaching of the Word of God is the centerpiece of this activity. According to Ephesians 4:11-16, God ordained elders to oversee this preaching and teaching:

> And he gave the apostles, the prophets, the evangelists, the shepherds and teachers, to equip the saints for the work of ministry, for building up the body of Christ, until we all attain to the unity of the faith and of the knowledge of the Son of God, to mature manhood, to the measure of the stature of the fullness of Christ, so that we may no longer be children, tossed to and fro by the waves and carried about by every wind of doctrine, by human

cunning, by craftiness in deceitful schemes. Rather, speaking the truth in love, we are to grow up in every way into him who is the head, into Christ, from whom the whole body, joined and held together by every joint with which it is equipped, when each part is working properly, makes the body grow so that it builds itself up in love.

According to Paul, unity occurs through instruction, and instruction occurs through the elders. We can go so far as to suggest that God ordained elders to put people "on the same page" with regard to what they believe and know about Jesus Christ. Without this elder-led instruction, the church will not mature into the measure of the stature of the fullness of Christ. Believers will then be at great risk of disunity, particularly with regard to doctrine and practice. Christians who are unwilling to receive elder-led instruction cannot be equipped for service within the body of Christ. A commitment to "getting on the same page" suggests that church membership is biblical.

Christians Are Accountable

According to Hebrews 13:17, Christians are accountable to the elders of the church. It is difficult to see how believers can obey the instructions found there if they are not members of particular churches:

> Obey your leaders and submit to them, for they are keeping watch over your souls, as those who will have to give an account. Let them do this with joy and not with groaning, for that would be of no advantage to you.

In the *Finishing Work* chapter, I made the case that a church is not a church unless it has elders, because the office is one of the marks of a particular church. Therefore, when God says that believers should submit to elders, we can infer that they are accountable to them within the context of particular churches. This implies that elders have God-given responsibility to exercise authority within those churches.

When believers hear about people having authority over other people in a church context, very reasonable questions arise. Some have observed or even experienced the abuse of such authority, and some have completely forsaken organized religion because of abuse at the hands of churches and church leaders. These leads us to ask several reasonable questions: Where does elder authority come from? What is the scope of this authority? What is the extent of this authority? And, how are believers to be protected from the abuse of authority?

Where Does Elder Authority Come From?

According to Ephesians 4:11, God gifted the church with the office of elder. According to Acts 20:28, the Holy Spirit made them elders. According to Hebrews 13:17, God will hold them accountable if they fail to watch out for the souls under their care. Therefore, elder authority comes from God.

However, God places people into church leadership through human instrumentality. Elders are usually selected by a vote of the congregation. This process is not infallible. Both churches and leaders can make grave mistakes. For this reason, God gives churches stringent criteria for selecting elders (1 Timothy 2; Titus 1), instructions for how elders should perform their responsibilities (1 Peter 5:1-2), and guidelines for how elders should be held accountable for their sins and failures (1 Timothy 5:17-22). These criteria, instructions, and guidelines would not be necessary if churches and leaders were infallible. Even though their authority comes from God, they have no right to abuse their authority, and the church can hold them accountable.

What is the Scope of Elder Authority?

It is unreasonable to think that church elders exercise authority over everyone they come into contact with. For instance, they have no authority over neighbors down the street, or strangers they encounter at a restaurant, or even people in other churches. It should be obvious that the people they oversee are those who have voluntarily placed themselves under the government and discipline of a particular church.

Church elders are not policemen with batons and handcuffs. Their only tools to exercise authority are the Word of God, the sacraments, and church discipline. As far as the visible church goes, submission to these tools is a voluntary obedience. Believers can choose to submit themselves according the will of God, or they can disregard the will of God and refuse.[15] It is therefore reasonable to assume that elder authority immediately extends only over those who have freely submitted themselves to their authority.[16] Paul calls these "all the flock, in which the Holy Spirit has made you overseers" (Acts 20:28). Peter uses the same language in 1 Peter 5:1-2. Elders are to "shepherd the flock of God that is among you." Clearly elders do not have authority over people who are not "among" them. Incidentally, this command is why elders are called *pastors,* because the word p*astor* comes from a word that means s*hepherd.*

Can you see how this fits into our case for church membership? Anyone can enjoy the benefits of attending church to a certain extent: strangers off the street, or occasional visitors, or even long-time attenders. But elders can only provide accountability to and be accountable for those who have willingly placed themselves under their care. It stands to reason then that elders must be able to distinguish between those who are under their care and those who are not. A church cannot oversee, discipline, or excommunicate someone otherwise. Therefore, the biblical mandate for government and discipline requires church membership or its functional equivalent.

What is the Extent of Elder Authority?

Everyone expects the elders to be about the business of running the church—administration, scheduling, budgets, etc. But if you are like most Westerners, you don't want people randomly intruding into things that are not their business. According to Scripture, however, elders do have authority to ask for obedience and submission. How much authority do they actually have? What are their limits?

Once again, the church does not have goon squads with baseball bats. Church leaders cannot force anyone to do anything. Unfortunately, I have known elders that exercise no authority whatsoever—permitting anything and everything—and elders who exercise far too much authority—intruding and prying into people's lives needlessly. For instance, I have heard of some who require pastoral permission before allowing someone to marry or take a job. We can safely say that elders have no business running the everyday lives and decisions of congregants. Such unusual intrusiveness violates the spirit of 1 Peter 5:1-2:

> So I exhort the elders among you . . . shepherd the flock of God that is among you, exercising oversight, not under compulsion, but willingly, as God would have you; not for shameful gain, but eagerly; not domineering over those in your charge, but being examples to the flock.

So over what then does their authority extend? According to Hebrews 13:17, elders are responsible for the souls under their care. The primary tool for this soul-care is the Word of God. Elders apply it through preaching, teaching, counseling, encouragement, admonition, and evangelism. Souls are spiritual, and elder authority is therefore spiritual in nature. It cannot be an "every detail of life" type of authority but must include people's spiritual well-being. Consequently, Scripture most clearly authorizes elder-authority over two specific areas of spiritual life.

Guarding the Flock against False Doctrine

In Acts 20:28-31, Paul commissioned the Ephesian elders to guard the flock against false doctrine:

> Pay careful attention to yourselves and to all the flock, in which the Holy Spirit has made you overseers, to care for the church of God, which he obtained with his own blood. I know that after my departure fierce wolves will come in among you, not sparing the flock; and from among your own selves will arise men speaking twisted things, to draw away the disciples after them. Therefore be alert, remembering that for three years I did not cease night or day to admonish every one with tears.

Elders are to protect the flock against those who distort the truth, who would enter in and tear the flock to pieces by teaching anything contrary to God's Word. The church has nothing if it does not have God's Word. It cannot make doctrine up out of thin air. If God's Word does not remain the church's constant touchstone, then the church becomes something other than the church—a synagogue of Satan. Getting the gospel right is life-giving. Getting it wrong is damning:

Galatians 1:8-9

> But even if we or an angel from heaven should preach to you a gospel contrary to the one we preached to you, let him be accursed. As we have said before, so now I say again: If anyone is preaching to you a gospel contrary to the one you received, let him be accursed.

The mainline denominations reveal the price for failing to guard the flock against doctrinal error.[17] Many of these churches have fallen into apostasy because they refused to preach the Word of God. To prevent this, elders must guard the doctrine of the church jealously by governing every aspect of what is taught throughout every level of the church. They must protect the flock against those who would preach anything other than the Word of God.

Guarding the flock Against Sin and Sinfulness

The other specific area of soul-care over which elders have clear authority is the area of sin and sinfulness. A church leader cannot care for souls without being concerned about sin in the lives of congregants. This is where the church leader's right and responsibility to exercise God-given authority can become uncomfortable for both leaders and those God has placed under their care.

Every Christian sins of course, even elders (more than you would like to know!). The church is filled with sinners, and elders should apply the healing balm of the Gospel to repentant sinners. But no Christian sins unrepentantly. Sometimes sinners are so willful and obstinate (aka *contumacious*) that the church must question their salvation. Under these circumstances and in order to guard the souls of both the sinner and the congregation, church leaders are ordained by God to require submission and obedience. Church leaders do this by confronting sin—addressing it privately when possible and publicly when necessary.

This is the most difficult aspect of a church leader's responsibility. No one likes being confronted, and no one enjoys confronting. If you're like me, you would much rather let people be. But that in itself would be a sin. Church leaders will be held accountable if they fail to watch out for souls, so they do not have the luxury of letting blatant and unrepentant sins continue.

But fear of judgment should not be their primary motivation. To allow unrepentant sin to continue would cause deep spiritual damage to the sinner and the church. The Bible teaches that unrepentant sin places souls in jeopardy (again, see Hebrews and 1 John). Anything that risks the judgment and damnation of the soul is by its very definition the responsibility of those who are ordained by God to care for souls. Elders cannot turn their heads when souls are at stake.

As we discussed in the previous chapter, elders do not exercise discipline with glee, or because they want to lord their authority, or because they like conflict. No one who does should be an elder. Rather, they exercise their authority because they recognize that they must care for souls. They must confront sin out of love and in hope of full repentance and restoration. The price of losing a soul is too great to ignore sin, both for the soul that is lost and for the leader that must give an account.

How Are Believers Protected from the Abuse of Authority?

The church has different levels of protection against elders who would abuse their authority. Again, none of these are infallible. But like the checks and balances built into the United States government, they serve to reduce the possibility of abuse and give churches options when it occurs.

Qualification

The first protection begins at the beginning—the selection of people who will be ordained to the office. Potential elders and pastors are always voted into office, which should give congregations a voice in who leads them.[18] People may aspire to the office (and that's a good thing according to 1 Timothy 3:1), but they should undergo examination and meet rigorous criteria. Paul told Timothy, "Do not be hasty in the laying on of hands," which refers to the practice of ordaining people to office (1 Timothy 5:22). If your church does not have a rigorous selection process or if it rotates through members just to fill empty leadership positions, then abuse of authority is much more likely.

In many denominations, pastoral candidates must undergo extensive examination, not just by a particular church but by a body of other elders outside that church. In presbyterian churches, this is done by the presbytery. Presbyterian pastoral candidates must undergo at least three years of seminary training, complete an internship, and take written and oral exams on their Christian experience and call to ministry, Bible knowledge, theology, church history, the sacraments, biblical languages, and presbyterian history, government, and discipline. Examinations take place before a committee first and then before the entire presbytery. Only after a candidate has been thoroughly vetted may he be ordained to a pastoral position. Similarly, congregational churches usually convene a large body of pastors and deacons from other churches to rigorously examine candidates before ordaining them.

Parity and Plurality

Another check and balance is that churches should have more than one elder (plurality), who are all equal (parity). This vests authority in the group rather than an individual. No one person holds authority over the church, but the entire group exercises authority as a unit.

Due Process: The Right to Hold Elders Accountable

First Timothy 5:19-21 implies that elders can be held accountable for their sins and failures. Unrepentant elders should be publicly rebuked:

> Do not admit a charge against an elder except on the evidence of two or three witnesses. As for those who persist in sin, rebuke them in the presence of all, so that the rest may stand in fear. In the presence of God and of Christ Jesus and of the elect angels I charge you to keep these rules without prejudging, doing nothing from partiality.

Due Process: Polymerization

Protection can also be had through the due process of connectional churches. Some denominations connect with other churches (remember a polymerized, plurality of particular churches?) to form a court system through which churches and individuals can appeal wrongs done to them by elders. If a problem is not addressed on the level of the particular church, it can be appealed to a higher court. In my own presbyterian denomination, these courts are taken very seriously and provide a high degree of accountability for elders.[19] What is more, in presbyterian denominations, teaching elders are not technically members of their particular churches. They are members of the presbytery, which means that they must answer to their brothers in the presbytery in addition to the particular churches they serve.

Obedient Christians Participate in the Sacraments

We have already argued in the *Finishing Work* chapter that the visible church meets together to administer baptism and partake of communion. Here we will focus primarily on communion. You will recall that because of what communion represents (union with Christ and his body), it should not be practiced outside the gathering of the visible church. Therefore, those who want to participate in communion should participate in the visible church in a way that honors what communion signifies.[20] Accordingly, those who refuse to participate in particular churches should not participate in communion.

Fencing the Table

What does communion have to do with membership? Can't a person just attend and participate in communion without becoming a member? To answer that question, we must return to the concept of *fencing the table,* which I briefly introduced earlier. *Fencing the table* occurs when a pastor explains who can and cannot participate in communion based upon Paul's warnings in 1 Corinthians 11:27-30:

> Whoever, therefore, eats the bread or drinks the cup of the Lord in an unworthy manner will be guilty concerning the body and

blood of the Lord. Let a person examine himself, then, and so eat of the bread and drink of the cup. For anyone who eats and drinks without discerning the body eats and drinks judgment on himself. That is why many of you are weak and ill, and some have died.

We call this *fencing the table* because it puts a "protective fence" around the table, not to protect the table, but to protect the participants. According to Paul, participating unworthily can be dangerous to both body and soul.

Preachers and denominations differ in the exact language they use, but most Gospel-preaching churches provide at least some word of warning. I am a presbyterian, but in my youth, I attended baptist churches that fenced the table as strongly as any church I have ever attended; so this is not just a presbyterian thing. When I oversee communion today, I usually fence the table with something similar to what I saw growing up. In fact, I usually use some form of these three invitations:

1. You may participate if you are united with Christ.
2. You may participate if you are united with the body of Christ.
3. You may participate if you are pursuing unity within the body of Christ.

United with Christ

The first invitation reflects the first of communion's two senses—it signifies union and communion with Christ. Once again, we get our word *communion* from the concept translated "participation" in 1 Corinthians 10:16.

Since the meal portrays, celebrates, and even practices our fellowship with Jesus Christ himself, only those who are united with Christ should participate. This means that the meal is only for those who are born-again believers. Those whose lives are characterized by sin in a way that causes them or the church to question their union with Christ should not participate. To this end, preachers will often warn that those living in unrepentant sin should abstain.

United with the Body of Christ

The second invitation reflects the second of communion's two senses—like a family meal around a table, it represents communion with those who are united together into the body of Christ, the visible church (1 Corinthians 10:17). Most pastors present this invitation as "You must be a member of a Gospel-preaching, Bible-believing church." Unless the church practices what is called *closed communion*, this usually means any such church, not just the one at which communion is being served.

You will recall that the church as a body distinguishes between those who are inside and those who are outside the church (1 Corinthians 5:9-13). The church cannot make this clear distinction apart from a membership process. Only those who are inside—united together into the visible church—should participate in communion. By restricting participation to members, churches are saying that those who refuse membership are refusing to be united together into the body of Christ. This second sense cannot be honored apart from a clear and consistent commitment to a particular church. How else do churches define this commitment apart from church membership?

Pursuing Unity within the Body of Christ

The third invitation is the logical conclusion of the first two. Communion with Christ and with the Body of Christ has very practical implications for those within the visible church. Paul wrote his communion-instructions because the Corinthians were violating the spirit of communion—treating each other horribly and creating divisions. Christians cannot participate in communion while refusing to demonstrate the unity the church is supposed to have in Christ. We learn this from the following passage:

1 Corinthians 11:17-22

> But in the following instructions I do not commend you, because when you come together it is not for the better but for the worse. For, in the first place, when you come together as a church, I hear that there are divisions among you. And I believe it in part, for there must be factions among you in order that those who are genuine among you may be recognized. When you come together, it is not the Lord's supper that you eat. For in eating, each one goes ahead with his own meal. One goes hungry, another gets drunk. What! Do you not have houses to eat and drink in? Or do you despise the church of God and humiliate those who have nothing? What shall I say to you? Shall I commend you in this? No, I will not.

Some disagree with the practice of fencing the table. They might even find it offensive:

> *"Why can't we just leave participation up to individuals to decide for themselves? What right do churches have to say who can participate and who cannot? Why is any of this the business of the church and its elders?"*

If all that I have already said in this and previous chapters does not make the answer to these questions obvious, then consider this: any sin significant enough to bring about illness or death is obviously a serious spiritual matter. That means that, as much or more than anything else I am aware of in the Bible, participation in communion falls directly under the purview of Hebrews 13:17—elders must watch and give account for the souls of the believers in their care, and believers must submit to that accountability. Without a doubt, communion is a soul matter, replete with fantastic spiritual benefits and great danger of spiritual judgment. If it does not fall under the category of "watch for their souls," then I do not know what does. Therefore, elders have the authority and responsibility to guard the communion table.

Having said that, I don't know of any elders that stand over people ready to slap the bread and wine out of their hands. Most churches pass the elements along rows or invite people to come to the front to pick them up. Participants decide for themselves, and elders do not make a scene. No one is ever singled out publicly apart from the final stages of church discipline. Elders will fence the table through verbal admonitions issued to all equally. It is up to individuals in attendance to examine their own hearts. Remember, the church does not have policemen with batons and handcuffs. This is a voluntary association. This is church membership.

Site Inspection

If you are a Christian, then you are a member of the church.

If you are a member of the invisible church, then you ought to be a member of the visible church.

You cannot be a member of the visible church without participating in a particular church.

You are not fully participating in a particular church unless you are participating in its privileges and responsibilities.

Part of the church can be seen, and part of it cannot. All believers belong to the part of the church that we cannot see, but the Bible presumes that those who are alive-and-well on planet earth will obediently participate in the part of the church that we can see. Those who do not participate in the visible church are either disobeying or are unaware of what the Bible teaches about the church we can see.

The part of the church that we can see—the visible church—comprises a polymerized plurality of particular churches. These churches can be connected together in different ways, but the doors to the visible church are always located in particular churches.

Christians can recognize particular churches by looking for the marks of the visible church: they have elders; they meet together for worship, instruction, and the sacraments; and they practice church discipline. Wherever these marks are found, so is the church.

Christians cannot participate in the privileges and responsibilities of the church without participating in particular churches. They cannot pursue unity, apply their God-given gifts, assemble for worship, instruction, and the sacraments, or submit to elders apart from participating in particular churches.

One final step in the case remains. We can see the church. We know what it looks like. We know what participating in it requires. Now we need to see how all this definitively adds up to church membership.

Group Study and Discipleship: Certificate of Occupancy

Scripture: 1 Cor. 12:14-27; Heb. 13:17; 1 Cor. 11:27-30; Ephesians 4:11-16

Discussion Questions:

1. Thinking through the construction metaphor, what's in this chapter that earns it the title "Certificate of Occupancy?"

2. On what does the author base his claim that Christians pursue unity?

3. What might a "Churchless Christian" say in response to the question, "How can a person who wants little to do with the visible church pursue unity within the visible church?"

4. The author implies that the domain for using God-given gifts is primarily the visible church. On what does he base this implication? Do you agree or disagree? Is it possible to refuse to use gifts within the visible body and fulfill the privileges and responsibilities of participation?

5. Who has been vested with primary responsibility for instructing other Christians?

6. According to Ephesians 4:11-16, what are the purposes and results of this instruction? Can these goals be accomplished outside the visible church?

7. Read Hebrews 13:17. Who is the verse addressed to? How might a Christian who stays outside the visible church explain this verse? Is there a venue outside the visible church in which this verse can be obeyed?

8. What else does communion signify besides union with Christ and his body?

9. Do you agree or disagree with the practice of fencing the table?

10. Concerning fencing the table, how would you answer the hypothetical questions on page 78: "Why can't we just leave participation up to individuals to decide for themselves? What right do churches have to say who can participate and who cannot? Why is any of this the business of the church and its elders?"

11. One of the implications of this chapter is that *you are not fully participating in a particular church unless you are participating in all its privileges and responsibilities.* Agree or disagree?

12. There may be other privileges and responsibilities of participation in the visible church other than the ones listed in this chapter. What would you add to or drop from the list if you were writing this chapter?

13. Can you state the argument for church membership that has been made so far in the book? What are its weak points and strong points? How would you improve it.

7

SITE CLEANUP

After the construction project is concluded, the worksite must be cleaned up. Debris, tools, supplies, and equipment are removed, and the building is made ready for people to move in. Accordingly, this chapter will clean up the case we have built by demonstrating that church membership is the inevitable conclusion of what the Bible teaches on the matter.

Hopefully, everything we have studied so far will convince "Churchless Christians" that they cannot remain disconnected from the church. They cannot stay outside and still be obedient to God's Word. This applies to *lone-wolf* Christians, *satellite* Christians, *parachurch* Christians, and *disgruntled* Christians.

But what about *The-Bible-Doesn't-Teach-Church-Membership* Christians? They probably agree with much of what has been presented here: the church should meet together, have officers, and practice discipline. They may be eager to participate in the church to a greater or lesser extent. But they fail to see how all this adds up to "You must join the church." Have we really built a strong case to active attenders who do not believe in membership?

If they have followed closely, they will have inferred that the privileges and responsibilities of participating in the church present some responsibilities for the church itself. The church cannot do much of what it is responsible to do apart from four key steps. These steps (or their functional equivalent) are the components of what we call church membership: Identification, Commitment, Reception, and Documentation.

Identification

In the *Finishing Work* chapter, we learned that churches distinguish between those who are Christians and those who are not—inside or outside, strangers or siblings in Christ. The church does this by evaluating their testimony of faith in Christ and baptizing them (or recognizing their baptism).

People enter the invisible church by being united to Christ through faith in his substitutionary work. Because they are in Christ, they are in the invisible church. Because they are in the invisible church, they should be in the visible church. They still have bodies after all. Because the doors to the visible church are located in particular churches, it is up to those churches to confirm their faith and baptism. Churches must therefore identify Christians.

Commitment

Before permitting someone to fully participate in the privileges and responsibilities of the visible church, a church must know that a prospective participant is committed to the worship, work, government, and discipline of that particular church. This commitment usually takes the form of making vows or signing a covenant. Examples of these can be found in the next chapter.

Commitment to the church and rejection of membership are mutually exclusive. Because government and discipline are essential to church life, a church obviously cannot welcome candidates into all its privileges and responsibilities if they are unwilling to commit to its government and discipline. But rejecting church membership rejects the government and discipline of the church. And rejecting government and discipline rejects the privileges and responsibilities of the church.

At the conclusion of the *Blueprint* chapter I mentioned a simple, logical test of commitment based on Hebrews 13:17. Imagine a husband and wife who attend a church but don't believe in membership. Instead they imagine they can be committed to the church's government and discipline apart from joining the church. So they tell this to the elders, and in response, the elders tell them they should join the church. Will they do it? If they refuse, can their commitment be taken seriously? Can they really disregard the first pastoral instruction of the church and still claim to be committed its government and discipline? In churches that practice membership, joining the church is not optional for those who desire to be committed to the government and discipline of the church.

Those who do not believe in church membership might respond that the elders' request is arbitrary. The elders might just as well have told them to "do twenty jumping jacks, because we said so." However, this objection goes out the window if we understand the biblical necessity of government and discipline. The request for membership is not arbitrary because a church must know who is under its care and who is not. So in the process of membership, the church simply asks for candidates to willingly and formally commit themselves to the government and discipline of the church.

Reception

The process of church membership also represents the formal recognition and reception of a candidate's commitment. By formally receiving the candidate, the church in turn makes its own commitment to the new member to provide the government, pastoral care, and accountability God has ordained within the visible church. A church can only commit to governing those who have committed themselves to its government, and it can only hold accountable those who have submitted themselves to its discipline. Once a church has received such a commitment, then—and only then—can the church receive the candidate into full participation. The church will then welcome them into all its privileges and responsibilities.

Documentation

Documentation may be a cold and sterile word, but it is a necessary step in the process. The church must identify, receive, and *remember* those who have committed themselves to the church. Therefore, documentation is simply the record of those whom the church has identified as baptized believers, who have committed themselves to the worship, work, government, and discipline of the church, and whose commitment has been recognized and received by the church. Without this record, membership is left to human whims and mere memory with all their faults and weaknesses.

In whatever ways membership is documented, the record at least consists of dates and names. Sometimes it will note professions of faith and baptisms. It may note whether members are "in good standing," which means they are not under discipline or have not been excommunicated. It may note whether they are communing or non-communing members.[21] These records become a part of the history of the visible church and stand firm across multiple generations. They allow the transfer of memberships from one church to another. They are important for the continuing government and discipline of the church.

Call it what you will. This process of identification, commitment, reception, and documentation is church membership. Those who ignore it disregard all the Bible has to say about unity, assembly, sacraments, worship, service, instruction, accountability, and more.

Group Study and Discipleship: Site Cleanup

Scripture: Heb. 13:17

Discussion Questions:

1. Thinking through the construction metaphor, what's in this chapter that earns it the title "Site Cleanup?"

2. On pages 28-30, the chapter reviews five types of Christians who are outside the visible church. Which of the five do think the argument of the book most effectively addresses? Least effectively? How would you improve the argument for these?

3. Are the components of church membership biblical (identification, commitment, reception, and documentation)? Which is the least grounded in Scripture? Does that mean it is unbiblical?

4. Can you rehearse the case for the church's responsibility to identify Christians?

5. Is documentation really necessary? Can you think of any way that a church could effectively practice identification, commitment, and reception *without* documentation?

6. Do you believe it is true that a church can only agree to hold accountable those who have submitted themselves to its discipline? Does the church have the right to hold accountable anyone who refuses to submit themselves to its discipline? If so, what are some examples and how would the church do that?

7. Occasionally the author uses the phrase "church membership or its functional equivalent." What might be an example that is functionally equivalent to church membership even though it is not called "church membership?" If a church does not

have church membership, can it biblically function without something that is its functional equivalent? Does the existence of a functional equivalent invalidate the argument for church membership?

8. For presbyterians: What is the distinction between communing and non-communing membership? Why do most presbyterians make this distinction? A small minority of presbyterians allow baptized children to participate in communion before they have made a profession of faith. Why might they do that? Why do most presbyterians believe they should not?

8

MOVING IN

We know who the builder is. We know the general shape of the building and how it is decked out. The building has been cleared for occupancy. Are you ready to move in? Do you see the need for church membership? Are you ready to begin the process of joining a church? If you are, here is what you need to know.

Be Sticky

What I mean by "be sticky" is that you should already come with everything necessary to stick to a church if at all possible. I get the phrase from my childhood—from those rubber, sticky, octopus-like toys that a child could send off for upon collecting enough cereal box tops. You could throw them at a wall and they would stick. I don't think cereal companies do that kind of thing anymore.

The point is, do not rely upon the church to be stickier than you. I know you want a friendly church, or one that feels right, or one that pursues you or bends over backward for you, but it is much more important that you be stickier than the church. Stickiness means that you know what you are looking for in a church and that you will do whatever it takes to locate and stick with a church once you find one. If you are not sticky, you will fall away once you realize how imperfect all churches are.

How friendly or welcoming a church is to first-time visitors is usually not the best criteria by which to evaluate a church. Any church can train members to introduce themselves and shake hands, but the ability to greet strangers with a smile is not the same thing as deep-seated Christian love.

Even the lack of such forwardness is not a great measure of what's going on inside a church. Many people—church-members and visitors alike—find it hard to be outgoing toward people they do not know. That's what makes some of those first visits hard for both you and the church. But if you know yourself, then you know the church—people are eager for others to see past first impressions to the heart within. An awkward first experience does not mean you or they are not loving and friendly. To really get to know them, you will need to stick with them for a while—to get comfortable with them, and let them get comfortable with you. A hand-shake and a friendly face is always nice, but it is simply not enough. So be sticky until you get to know some people.

Pick a Church

My case for church membership has not covered everything you should consider when picking a church. However, I will draw a couple of guidelines from what I have already presented and then suggest some guiding questions you can ask before joining a church.

According to this book, if the "church" you are considering does not meet together, practice discipline, or have elders, then take it off your list. It is not a church.[22] Beyond these, you should at least pick a church that is unified, that truly worships, that preaches nothing but God's Word, that faithfully baptizes and shares communion, and that welcomes the use of gifts and abilities. You may also want to consider these guiding questions:

1. What does the church expect of its members?
2. What is the church's denomination?
3. Do you believe the church's government is structurally biblical?
4. Can you trust the elders? Are they knowledgeable, pastoral, and available?
5. Does the church connect itself with other churches? How?
6. What is the church's theology, creed, or confession? Is it Reformed? Arminian? Something in between?
7. Are the sermons more topical or expositional?
8. Does the pastor's preaching encourage, convict, and strengthen you?
9. Does the church evangelize? Does it support missions?
10. Does the church pray and encourage prayer?
11. Does the church meet the needs of people in the congregation?
12. Does the church minister to the community?
13. Does the church minister to your entire family?
14. Is the church too big? Too small?

Many more questions can and should arise as you pick a church. Some of them will not be answered in ways you would prefer. That is okay, because you are sticky and no church is perfect. Some churches lack resources, or are just starting out, or are doing the best they can. Maybe a church needs you in order to make up for what it lacks.

Check your Qualifications

So what are the qualifications for church membership? Of course, every church or denomination is different, but most churches (good ones at least) are concerned with at least three qualifications for church membership:

1. Are you a Christian?
2. Have you been baptized?
3. Are you willing to commit yourself to the privileges and responsibilities of the church?

How churches determine the answers to these questions varies from church to church. What follows are some common practices of protestant, bible-believing churches in North America. The church you are interested in may differ.

Tell a Church Officer You Are Ready to Join

The church membership process usually begins by letting a church officer know that you are interested in joining the church. If you have decided to join a church, it is likely that you have attended there for some time already. Hopefully, you now know a few church members who would be glad to introduce you to a church officer, like a deacon, elder, or pastor. Some churches have invitations after their sermons during which they invite potential members to come forward. A church officer will be waiting at the front to walk you through the process. Regardless, talking with a church officer is usually the place to start. Some churches print information on how to join the church in the Sunday bulletin. They may ask you to fill out and turn in a form, in which case a church officer will likely contact you to continue the process.

Take a Membership Class (or Equivalent)

Many churches require candidates to attend membership classes. These classes will probably last several weeks and will cover everything you need to know about the church. You will learn how to know that you are truly a Christian and why baptism is important. The teacher will discuss what is unique about their church, including important doctrines and denominational beliefs. They will acquaint you with the mission and ministries of the church and describe ways that you can become involved. They will probably also go over what they expect of members by acquainting you with the membership vows you will be taking or the church covenant you will be signing. They will probably walk you through the process of examination that will come next. Smaller churches may not hold official membership classes, but a good church will find a way to acquaint you with all these things before you make a final decision to join the church. If they do not, be sure to ask plenty of questions so that you can make the most informed decision possible.

Join by Profession of Faith

After you talk with the church officer, you will be scheduled to meet with those in the congregation who are responsible for evaluating your profession of faith. Their concern, of course, is to determine whether you are a Christian. They will probably ask you to describe how you became a Christian and when you were baptized. They will want to know that your life is not characterized by any sin that should call your faith into question. If you have not been baptized yet, they may schedule a baptismal service, which should be a very exciting event.

Giving a testimony in public is not always easy. Some people do not know how to put their faith into words. If you have attended a membership class, the church has hopefully helped you do that. Not everyone can say exactly when God saved them, but churches are most concerned with knowing whether you understand and believe that Jesus died for your sins and that you are not relying upon your own goodness and good works to earn your relationship with God. They want to know that you are committed to Christ and taking your faith very seriously. They may ask about your gifts and what you expect of church and how you expect to serve the church. Most churches are very generous in their acceptance of a person's profession of faith, knowing that only God truly knows the heart.

The ones responsible for evaluating your profession of faith may be church officers or the entire congregation. If it is the entire congregation, be aware that they will probably ask you to give a brief testimony of your salvation and baptism in front of the entire church. Hopefully the church leadership will help you prepare for this. After hearing your testimony, the deciding body will then take a vote to receive you into membership.

Join by Letter of Transfer

Instead of joining by profession of faith, sometimes people join by "letter of transfer." This means that they were already members of another church. Perhaps they moved to a different area and have found a new church. Instead of joining by profession of faith, they choose to simply transfer their membership. In this case, the church they are joining may contact the church they just left and ask for a letter of transfer, or the church they are joining may rely upon candidates to request a letter of transfer. You can ask the church leadership which they prefer.

If you are a "member in good standing" the letter should be sent right away. To be a member in good standing is to not be under church discipline. Churches generally have a "gentleman's agreement" that they will not receive into membership people who are under discipline in other congregations. This keeps people from running away by hopping churches. If a church refuses to send a letter or says that you are under discipline, candidates are free to make a case that their discipline was unjustified and ask to join by profession of faith. It is up to the receiving body to decide whether they will receive people into membership who are under discipline elsewhere.

Some denominations will not transfer letters to different denominations. For example, baptist and presbyterian churches might not transfer letters to each other. In this case, you can still join by profession of faith.[23]

Take Vows and Sign Covenants

Before you join, find out if the church expects you to take vows or sign a church covenant. You will want to study these beforehand so that you can know exactly what you are agreeing to. Taking a vow is no small thing, and the Scriptures warn against rashness. Vows represent your promise to God and to the rest of the believers in the congregation. If you cannot in good conscience make those promises then you should not join the church.

In most churches these vows are made in front of the entire congregation. To give you a sense of how serious they may be, here are the vows that are taken by those who join any churches in my own presbyterian denomination:

> Do you acknowledge yourselves to be sinners in the sight of God, justly deserving His displeasure, and without hope save in His sovereign mercy?
>
> Do you believe in the Lord Jesus Christ as the Son of God, and Savior of sinners, and do you receive and rest upon Him alone for salvation as He is offered in the Gospel?
>
> Do you now resolve and promise, in humble reliance upon the grace of the Holy Spirit, that you will endeavor to live as becomes the followers of Christ?

Do you promise to support the church in its worship and work to the best of your ability?

Do you submit yourselves to the government and discipline of the church, and promise to study its purity and peace?

Instead of vows, many baptistic churches require member candidates to sign a church covenant. A covenant is an agreement that spells out what a church expects of its members. Those who sign are making a commitment to meet those expectations. Here is a sample covenant borrowed (with permission) from Capitol Hill Baptist Church in Washington DC:[24]

> Having, as we trust, been brought by divine grace to repent and believe in the Lord Jesus Christ and to give up ourselves to him, and having been baptized upon our profession of faith, in the name of the Father and of the Son and the Holy Spirit, we do now, relying on His gracious aid, solemnly and joyfully renew our covenant with each other.
>
> We will work and pray for the unity of the Spirit in the bond of peace.
>
> We will walk together in brotherly love, as becomes the members of a Christian Church, exercise an affectionate care and watchfulness over each other and faithfully admonish and entreat one another as occasion may require.
>
> We will not forsake the assembling of ourselves together, nor neglect to pray for ourselves and others.
>
> We will endeavor to bring up such as may at any time be under our care, in the nurture and admonition of the Lord, and by a pure and loving example to seek the salvation of our family and friends.
>
> We will rejoice at each other's' happiness and endeavor with tenderness and sympathy to bear each other's burdens and sorrows.

We will seek, by Divine aid, to live carefully in the world, denying ungodliness and worldly lusts, and remembering that, as we have been voluntarily buried by baptism and raised again from the symbolic grave, so there is on us a special obligation now to lead a new and holy life.

We will work together for the continuance of a faithful evangelical ministry in this church, as we sustain its worship, ordinances, discipline, and doctrines. We will contribute cheerfully and regularly to the support of the ministry, the expenses of the church, the relief of the poor, and the spread of the Gospel through all nations.

We will, when we move from this place, as soon as possible, unite with some other church where we can carry out the spirit of this covenant and the principles of God's Word.

May the grace of the Lord Jesus Christ, and the love of God, and the fellowship of the Holy Spirit be with us all. Amen.

Group Study and Discipleship: Moving In

Scripture: 1 Cor. 12:14-27; Heb. 13:17; 1 Cor. 11:27-30

Discussion Questions:

1. What's in this chapter that earns it the title "Moving In?"

2. How do the steps for joining a church in this chapter compare to the steps for membership in the congregation you are currently participating in? If your church was writing these steps, how would they be different, or what would else would it include?

3. Take some time to review the questions on page 93 with your mentor/group leader. What other questions would you add to these?

4. Compare the sample vows and covenant. Which do you prefer and why?

5. Is there anything left out of the vows or covenant you think should be included? Should anything be excluded?

9

PUNCH LIST

In keeping with our construction metaphor, this chapter is called "The Punch List." A punch list is a final list of problems that need fixed after construction is complete. It lists the scratches and dents that are the inevitable result of workers traipsing around a job site, such as gashes in freshly painted walls or dings in doorframes. Our punch list could include many unresolved questions that may have come to mind, but I am concerned here to address only one: the problem of differences, disagreements, and denominations in the visible church. If the church is supposed to be unified, why are there so many denominations?

The reason this topic comes up in a book on church membership is that the fractured state of the visible church sometimes underlies people's rejection of "organized religion." They use it as a justification to avoid committing themselves to the visible church. A church that appears to preach hundreds of competing truths can hardly speak authoritatively to a culture that is already suspicious of claims to absolute truth. Why are there so many churches? So many denominations? So many differences? So many disagreements? To paraphrase Scripture, "a double-minded religion is unstable in all its ways." How can our relativistic culture take the church's truth claims seriously if all it sees are competing claims?

This chapter will acknowledge the problem of differences, disagreements, and denominations. But it will attempt to show that the church is not as divided as it may seem. In fact, there are understandable reasons for our disagreements and differences. And instead of hurting the church, denominations actually create unity out of diversity.

The Ideal of Unity

As we have seen, unity is a reoccurring theme in biblical texts about the church. We built our case for church membership upon our union with Christ: Since Christians are united with Christ, they should be united with the body of Christ, the visible church. The Body Illustration repeatedly reinforces the ideal of unity—within the body, all Christians should use their gifts in unity with one another. Everywhere you look in Scripture, the church is supposed to be unified. Accordingly, one cannot pursue unity apart from an accountable commitment to a particular church. This is what we have called *church membership*. Living the Christian life apart from the body and pursuing unity within the body are not compatible courses of action. Unity is fundamental to the church and to our case for church membership.

The Reality of Disunity

How is this belief in unity consistent with the division that apparently afflicts the visible church throughout world? With over 200 denominations and 300,000 congregations in the United States alone, how can we say that the visible church is in any way unified?

Differences and disagreements are a very real problem. Christians, churches, and denominations frequently wage sinful wars with one another. Churches and denominations split. People get hurt. Hurting people run away from churches, compounding the disunity caused by differences and disagreements. This problem is not new. Even in the church's earliest forms, differences and disagreements plagued the church. If the early church had *really* been unified, Paul and the other Scripture-writers would not have focused so much time and effort on the topic of unity.

Nevertheless, the testimony of Scripture is that the church accomplished its mission in spite of these disagreements and differences. The Jerusalem Council resolved "no small dissension and debate" by conveying a consensus judgment to the church through a letter (Acts 15:1-29). Paul confronted Peter to his face for compromising with the Judaizers in Antioch (Galatians 2:11-14). We can presume that Peter repented, and their relationship and cooperation in the Gospel continued (II Peter 3:15-16). And, of course, Paul and Barnabas famously disagreed regarding whether Mark should accompany them. Although they parted ways, the result doubled their missionary efforts as they headed off in different directions (Acts 15:36-41). At some point Paul's confidence in Mark was restored (II Timothy 4:11). These examples demonstrate God working in, through, and despite disagreements in the church.

As difficult as it must have been to maintain unity then, today's church is larger and has its own unique issues. It has been divided over the centuries by differences of authority, interpretation, opinion, practice, and doctrine. Issues, circumstances, and cultures have changed radically. Models of ministry exemplified by the early church are now seemingly more difficult and less practical to apply. Until Christ settles all our differences when he returns, a single, world-wide, visible, doctrinally-united church is impractical and maybe even impossible.

More Unified Than You Think

But the church has always been more unified than may appear on the surface. Flowing down the middle of Christianity is a broad river of shared beliefs and practices. Christians almost universally accept the earliest statements of belief—the Apostles Creed (ca. 200 A.D.) and the Nicene Creed (325 A.D). After millennia, churches around the world still quote these every Sunday. Since the Reformation in the 1500's, thousands upon thousands of churches have united around the reformed creeds and confessions—the Westminster Confession of faith, the London Baptist Confession, the Belgic Confession, the Heidelberg Catechism, the Canons of Dort, the Thirty-Nine Articles. All these share a common reformed theology that creates a strong sense of brotherhood and affection across countless denominations.

The church has also been united in its moral beliefs—the sanctity of life and marriage, justice for the oppressed, and provision for the poor, orphaned, widowed, and infirm. Christianity's beliefs and practices remain massively monolithic, which means the visible church is united in ways that many critics refuse to acknowledge.

Within the particular stream for which this book was written—evangelical Protestantism[25]—our churches and denominations get little credit for the ways in which we are unified. We are united in our acceptance of the fundamentals of the faith. We are united in our belief that salvation is by grace through faith alone in the person and work of Jesus Christ. We are united in our commitment to the inspiration and authority of the Word of God.

It is true that doctrines and practices often separate us into different groups, and some divide more than others (each church and denomination determines how important its own differences are). Regardless, many churches still work closely together as long as they are not forced to compromise. Complete unity may not always be possible, but churches throughout evangelical Protestantism recognize the importance of working across boundaries for the sake of unity.

The Reason for Disunity

As important as it is to acknowledge the church's unity, disunity is still a very real problem. The reason for disunity in the visible church is twofold: 1) we are sinful, and 2) we are finite.

Sinfulness

To be a sinner means that we are governed to greater or lesser degrees by our sinfulness. We have a heart condition that leads us into selfishness with regard to love and disobedience with regard to law. We know what is right, yet we fail to do it. Even at our best, we struggle to get along with others, and we even struggle with those who are struggling, hurting, or wounded. We are easily overcome by emotion—by rage, by fear, by jealousy—and we fail to respond to others in Christ-like ways. Sometimes the way we respond is more devilish than Christian. We all know stories of Christians who behaved nothing like what one should expect. Some of us can even testify that the people who have hurt us most in life called themselves Christians. So sinfulness definitely gets in the way of unity. Though we have been set free from slavery to sin, some sinfulness remains, and it will not be entirely eradicated until Christ returns. Too many give in to that remaining sin, failing to avail themselves of the means of their sanctification, and seek to satiate sinful desires in ways that cause conflict (James 4:1-7). Our sinfulness is a massive root of disunity. Where sin is the cause of disunity, the church owes it to Christ to repent and reconcile.

Finiteness

The second reason complete unity is not possible is not itself evil. It is built into who we are as God's creatures—we are finite. God made us that way from the start. We say that God is *infinite*—he knows everything, he is everywhere, and he has all power (among other things). We on the other hand have definite boundaries. We are *finite* by our very nature. God set limits to our knowledge, presence, and power when he created us.

Sin may have made these limitations worse, but even without it we would still be limited by our finiteness. Before the Fall, God declared his finite creation good. Back then, Adam and Eve were united in their knowledge of God until the Fall. But they were still finite, and even in an unfallen world differences would likely have arisen. We cannot know how God would have maintained the unity of an unfallen, finite humanity. But finiteness by itself is not a sin problem. So today, when disagreements and differences are the result of our finiteness, they do not have to be sinful. No church knows everything, and all are responsible for what they believe to be God's claims upon their own consciences. Even when sin is taken out of the equation, disagreements and differences are still the necessary consequence of our finiteness.

Differences over doctrine, practice, opinion, and preference make the biblical ideal nearly impossible. No system of belief or practice is perfect, especially since all are implemented by sinful, finite people. But that does not mean that we should not strive for as much unity as is practical or possible. Jesus prayed that all his followers throughout all ages would be united together (John 17). Paul called upon Christians to demonstrate unity in their individual churches by loving, serving, cooperating, and deferring to one another (I Corinthians 1:10-16; 12:12-27; Ephesians 4:1-4). Somehow, Christians are expected to show the true unity of the body of Christ in visible ways, even though the church is made up of many different particular churches. The primary way most churches do that is through denominational affiliation.

The Benefits of Denominations

The word *denomination* has a couple of different uses. It can refer to a label for specific beliefs and practices or it can refer to the names of specific groups or organizations. Differing beliefs and practices are called *denominational distinctives*. For example, presbyterians are ruled by a plurality of elders, connect themselves with other presbyterian churches, and baptize babies. Baptists only baptize believers by immersion and believe that each particular church is sovereign over its own affairs. Thus, broad denominational labels like baptist and presbyterian are useful because they help us quickly identify churches and their distinctives.

When a *denomination* refers to a specific group or organization, it will usually have a proper name. Specific presbyterian denominations include the Presbyterian Church (USA), Presbyterian Church in America, Orthodox Presbyterian Church, and Associate Reformed Presbyterian Church, to name only a few. Baptist denominations include the Southern Baptist Convention, American Baptist Churches USA, the General Association of Regular Baptist Churches, and so on. By the way, baptist groups usually do not think of themselves as *denominations* because each church is technically independent from all the others. But since they still function like denominations, the rest of the world tends to think of them as such.

Just like an individual cannot pursue unity apart from a particular church (membership), a particular church cannot pursue unity apart from some real connection to other churches (polymerization). Because particular churches are the building blocks of the visible church, the best opportunity for particular churches to pursue unity within the visible body of Christ is through denominational affiliation.

Therefore denominations do not have to be a bad thing. In light of our sinfulness and finiteness, they can be a good and necessary means to unify, diversify, and rectify the visible church.

Denominations Unify the Visible Church

In John 17 Christ prays that his future followers would be united *and* that they would be sanctified in the truth. Together, these two petitions foreshadow a potential conflict between unity and fidelity. Anytime Christians stand firm on their convictions concerning the truth, unity with those who disagree will be very difficult. But denominations help resolve this problem. They evidence believers' concern for the fulfillment of both these petitions together. They unite churches with other churches that share the same convictions concerning the truth. As one theologian says, "Denominations are intended to be a balance between cooperation and conviction."[26]

All around the world and throughout history, protestant churches have united as much as their differences will allow. They have formed denominations that demonstrate unity in different ways. Some have established hierarchies of bishops and priests (Prelacy). Some base their model upon the elders and councils of the early church (Presbyterianism). Others assemble together in annual conventions or meetings or join like-minded churches in loose associations (Partnerships). Regardless of how it is done, the biblical doctrine of unity suggests that it is appropriate for individual churches to visibly connect themselves to the larger church by some means.

Denominationalism is therefore an example of both particularization *and* polymerization, each of which are essential aspects of the visible church. The existence of separate denominations cannot negate the unity of the church any more than the existence of separate particular churches. If every individual congregation is the church (particularization), then every individual denomination is also the church (polymerization). Just like "the whole is found in each place," the whole is also found in each denomination.[27] Therefore, denominations help unify the church.

Denominations Diversify the Visible Church.

Because Christians are sinful and finite, we should not expect to find total truth or perfect practice in only one church or denomination. Thus different denominations will naturally have diverse emphases and practices. According to I Corinthians 12:12, the church is made of many parts, and "all its many parts form one body. So it is with Christ." Paul applies his "members of the body" analogy to both the broad categories of Gentiles and Jews and to the narrower category of local congregations (12:13; cf. Ephesians 2: 11-21). This range of both broad and narrow suggests that the analogy could apply above and beyond the level of the local congregation, namely that different denominations within the visible church are important expressions of both the unity and the diversity that God has built into the body of Christ. What the church lacks in one denomination, it may very well possess in another. Therefore, denominations diversify the church.

Denominations Rectify the Visible Church

Denominational diversity provides the parts that together make the whole. The church therefore possesses a sort of internal accountability—the parts provide checks-and-balances. So, counter-intuitively, the apparent schism of different denominations may be the best mechanism to unite the church as much as is practical in a fallen, finite world. A church that holds itself accountable within and across denominations will maintain a stronger allegiance to God and his Word than one that has no accountability. Even when older protestant denominations leave off preaching God's Word, denominationalism keeps them from taking the rest of the church with them. On the contrary, many faithful denominations continue to grow as liberal ones lose millions of members. And as old denominations fall into unbelief, new denominations continue to form, always calling the faithful together to maintain allegiance to God and his Word.

The Roman Catholic Church illustrates the dangers of a "homogenous" church without checks-and-balances. The more the Roman church consolidated its power to control its people, the more corrupt and unbiblical it became. The church already had the Bible, but schism was still a constant threat. So the organization required something in addition to the Bible—human beings who could claim infallible authority in the name of God. This "magisterium" gradually took control and things then began to go very badly for the church as a whole. It took hundreds of years and the Protestant Reformation to restore the Scriptures as the only infallible authority for faith and practice. The Reformation decentralized the church's authority and introduced denominations to the world. The church has been better for it ever since.

Since a one-world visible church is not possible this side of eternity (remember—the church failed miserably with that experiment), denominationalism is the best, most providential option. A church with many different denominations is more likely to teach, preach, and worship with a higher degree of unity within and across those denominations than any amalgam constantly mired in debilitating chaos and division.

A Potential Problem with Non-Denominationalism

Some churches claim to be non-denominational. Non-denominational churches exist for different reasons. They might not want any other church or organization telling them what to believe or do. They may not want to scare people away or turn people off with denominational distinctives. They might believe that denominationalism reflects poorly upon the church in the eyes of the world. They might argue that denominations divide the church in the fashion of "I am of Paul; I am of Apollos." In spite of these reasons, close examination often reveals them to still be denominational in the broadest sense of the word. They only lack a label. In other words, they are baptist without claiming to be baptist, or pentecostal without claiming to be pentecostal. They have denominational distinctives; they just do not want those distinctives to be at the forefront of their identity. By downplaying their differences, they believe they will better fulfill the biblical expectation of unity.

Unfortunately, non-denominationalism does not solve the apparent problem of disagreements, differences, and denominations. It even has the potential to undermine its own interest in unity. To be totally unaffiliated with or unaccountable to any other church or group of churches makes unity a mere theory without practical application beyond what any one church decides for itself. The refusal to join a denomination is much more atomistic and disunified than denominationalism.

So what would a non-denominational church have to do if it wanted to take unity seriously? It would have to connect itself to the larger church while either diluting its core beliefs to near meaninglessness or clearly specifying and standing behind its doctrinal convictions. To do the latter would result in a sort of *ipso facto* denominationalism. Such an exclusive act would undermine the premise of non-denominationalism. All the church would lack is a label to match its core beliefs. There are plenty to pick from. No need to pretend any longer.

The counter-argument that "doctrine divides" ignores the truth that unity without doctrine is not really unity. Ironically, the core beliefs that unite Christianity were often settled through intense conflict. The visible church's battles separated the orthodox from the heretical. Doctrine was often divisive, but in many cases that proved to be a good thing

On the other hand, the first option—diluting beliefs—guts unity of any real meaning. If non-denominational churches must dilute their beliefs in order to unite with the larger church, what exactly are they willing to give up to make their beliefs more agreeable to others? What of others' beliefs will they ignore? Who among them will tell others their beliefs are unimportant and must be sacrificed for the sake of unity? Or better, who would accept this demand from others toward themselves?

Denominationalism,. then, is what unity looks like when the Golden Rule is practiced in the visible church. It is some-in-the-Church treating others-in-the-Church as they would want to be treated. More than fighting over differences, denominations unite the church around key distinctives. In a finite and fallen world, denominationalism is thus a necessary and beneficial means to create unity in a church filled with diversity.[28]

Group Study and Discipleship: Punch List

Scripture: John 17; Ephesians 1:10;

Discussion Questions:

1. Thinking through the construction metaphor, what's in this chapter that earns it the title "Punch List?"

2. Why are differences, disagreements, and denominations relevant to a discussion of church membership?

3. The author has applied the following sentence to a Christian's church membership: "Living the Christian life apart from the body and pursuing unity within the body are not compatible courses of action." In what ways might that also apply to a church's denominational membership or affiliation?

4. Give examples of problematic disunity in the church around the world. Is disunity ever a good thing? Can you think of instances, either biblical or extrabiblical, where God used disunity for good?

5. What are two listed reasons the church experiences disunity? Can you think of more?

6. Imagine a world in which the Fall never occurred and sin is not a problem but in which we still are and ever will be finite creatures. How might God maintain unity in an unfallen world filled with finite creatures (for instance, in the New Heavens and Earth following the resurrection)?

7. In spite of differences, in what ways is the visible church united in its doctrinal beliefs? In its moral beliefs? In what ways are the churches from different denominations in your town doctrinally and morally similar?

8. What are three listed benefits of denominationalism for the visible church? Can you think of others?

9. What would happen in the visible church without denominations? Is it possible for the visible church to have unity apart from denominations? What would have to happen for the church to be unified apart from denominations? What might the connectional structure and beliefs of that church look like?

10. What do you think of non-denominationalism? Have you ever been a part of a non-denominational church? How did that church connect itself to the larger church?

11. What does the author mean when he says that "denominationalism is what unity looks like when the Golden Rule is practiced in the visible church?"

10

FINAL INSPECTION

The job is finished. As I said in the preface, this case for membership originated in very personal and pastoral circumstances. I needed to build this to fill my own knowledge-gap. But I firmly believe the church has also needed a freshly constructed case for church membership. It has relied far too long on tradition and utilitarianism. It has needed to ground membership in Scripture.

Whether or not this case is quality construction will be left for others to decide. I hope they will test it out. Examine the nooks and crannies. Live in it a while. Offer improvements. Renovate. Maybe even build a better case. May they remember, however, that apart from a scriptural foundation, fresh construction will eventually collapse.

As we leave the site, we will take one last glance over what has been built. I have prayed it is solid. I have tried to build it on the strongest possible foundation—the Word of God. I want it to last.

Here is the final site inspection:

If you are a Christian, then you are a member of the church.

If you are a member of the invisible church, then you ought to be a member of the visible church.

You cannot be a member of the visible church without participating in a particular church.

You are not fully participating in a particular church unless you are participating in its privileges and responsibilities.

You cannot fully participate in the privileges and responsibilities of a particular church apart from the process of identification, commitment, reception, and documentation.

Part of the church can be seen, and part of it cannot. All believers belong to the part of the church that we cannot see, but the Bible presumes that those who are alive-and-well on planet earth will obediently participate in the part of the church that we can see. Those who do not participate in the visible church are either disobeying or are unaware of what the Bible teaches about the church we can see.

The part of the church that we can see—the visible church—comprises a polymerized plurality of particular churches. These churches can be connected together in different ways, but the doors to the visible church are always located in particular churches.

Christians can recognize particular churches by looking for the marks of the visible church: they have elders; they meet together for worship, instruction, and the sacraments; and they practice church discipline. Wherever these marks are found, so is the church.

Christians cannot participate in the privileges and responsibilities of the church without participating in particular churches. They cannot pursue unity, apply their God-given gifts, assemble for worship, instruction, and the sacraments, or submit to elders apart from participating in particular churches. Christians cannot fully participate in the privileges and responsibilities of the church without confirming their union with Christ, committing themselves to the worship, work, government, and discipline of the church, and being received into the body by the church. The record of this process is called church membership. Church membership is therefore accountable commitment to a particular church.

Group Study and Discipleship: Final Inspection

Scripture: Rom. 12:3-8; Eph. 4:1-16; 1 Cor. 12:12-31

Discussion Questions:

1. For review, what are the two broadest categories that apply to the church (the Blueprint)?

2. What is the Body Illustration? What are the three most extensive passages?

3. What three words that begin with P describe the frame or shape of the church that you can see in this world?

4. List three ways the visible church can be connected (also starting with P).

5. What are the three historical marks of the visible church? And how do they compare to the three marks this book presents?

6. List five privileges and responsibilities of the visible church.

7. On a scale of 1-5, weak to strong, how strong is the case for membership this book has built? How biblical? What are its weakest points? What are its strongest points? How would you improve it?

8. How confident are you that church membership is more than just a tradition or useful practice? Do you feel you could explain the case for church membership?

9. Reread each of the quotes that begin chapter one. Taking each quote in turn, what have you learned that you could use in response to each of the quotes? Be as specific as possible in your argument. What Bible verses would you take the speaker to?

ABOUT THE AUTHOR

Dr. Dennis Eldon Bills is an ordained minister in the New River Presbytery of the Presbyterian Church in America. He received a BA and MA from Bob Jones University, an MEd from Covenant College, and a DMin from Pittsburgh Theological Seminary. As a rural Appalachian minister, he works bi-vocationally as an educator, family law mediator, and businessman. He and his wife Kathi have three grown sons.

Dennis has also published *How to Preach with an Interpreter* (Wipf and Stock, 2010)*, The Captives of Abb's Valley: Revised and Annotated* (ReformingWV Publications, 2019), and *Presbyterianism in West Virginia: A History* (ReformingWV Publications, 2019), as well as the first, more presbyterian edition of this book. He can be reached at dbills@adoniram.net.

ENDNOTES

[1] Scripture presents a beautiful array of illustrations to help us understand this union. In *Redemption Accomplished and Applied,* John Murray says that *union with Christ* is like the union that exists between the persons of the Trinity (John 14:23; 17:21-23) or between Adam and all the human race (Romans 5:12-19; I Corinthians 15:19-49); the union that exists between man and wife (Ephesians 5:22-23); the relationship of the vine to the branches (John 15) or between the stones of a building and the chief cornerstone (Ephesians 2:19-22; I Peter 2:4-5); and the union that exists between the head and the other parts of the human body (Ephesians 4:15-16). The Bible uses each of them to shed different rays of light on what it means to be united with Christ.

[2] Read especially Romans, Corinthians, Ephesians, and Colossians and take note of all the references to the body of Christ. 1 Corinthians 12, Ephesians 4, and Romans 12 contain the most detailed versions. We will look at those in more detail shortly.

[3] This is from the Westminster Confession of Faith (25:2). The idea of *catholic* is older than the Roman Catholic Church. It is just another word for *universal.* The clause "and of their children" reflects the Presbyterian origins and convictions of the Confession. For those who are not Presbyterians and who do not believe that children are members of the Visible Church until baptism, the main point of the paragraph—that there is no ordinary possibility of salvation outside the visible church—still stands. Non-Presbyterians need to understand that Presbyterians DO NOT believe that baptism regenerates souls or remits sins—that the baptized children of believers still need to be born again and profess faith in Christ.

[4] Millard J. Erickson, *Christian Theology* (Grand Rapids, MI: Baker Book House, 1985), 1026.

[5] The Westminster Confession of Faith (WCF) is not the Bible, and therefore does not carry its authority. However, it is a widely-accepted, historical expression of what the Bible teaches. It originated in the 1600s and is still the official "statement of faith" for presbyterian churches. All churches have creeds and confessions, whether they are stated or unstated, old or new, short or long. Few are as time-tested and widely received as the WCF. The Baptists have their own version called the London Baptist Confession of Faith. It is almost as old and borrows heavily from the WCF.

[6] In Presbyterianism, the children of believers are baptized into the church even though they do not yet possess personal faith in Jesus Christ. They are known as non-communing members because they cannot yet participate in communion. Later, when their faith is confirmed by the church, they are admitted to communion on the basis of their own faith in Christ and the church's confidence in their profession of faith.

[7] In what follows, I try not to argue for one over another. Obviously I would not be presbyterian if I did not believe it was most biblical. But I understand that good churches disagree and thus want to present the options as non-prejudicially as

possible. This is, of course, a very simplified presentation of the options. Church structures can get very complex.

[8] In the mouths of protestants, p*relacy* is often a pejorative term. But it starts with a "p" and conveys my meaning, so I use it anyway. But as a Presbyterian, I must confess that I don't object to its negative connotations. So much for presenting without prejudice.

[9] See any number of systematic theologies, like Berkhof, 577-578. Take note that Mark Dever has taken similar liberties with his "Nine Marks of a Healthy Church."

[10] The other is the office of deacon. The word *deacon* means *servant*. We know it was also an office because its qualifications immediately follow those of the office of elder in 1 Timothy 3. Deacons are usually responsible for the practical, hands-on aspects of running the visible church, like mercy ministries and maintaining buildings and grounds. Their primary responsibility is to ensure that the material needs of the congregation are met so that the elders can devote themselves to pastoring the church without distraction. The story of how the office of deacon began is found in Acts 6:1-7.

[11] Elwell, Walter A. *Evangelical Dictionary of Biblical Theology* (Grand Rapids, MI: Baker Books, 1998), "Church."

[12] For why they are wrong, see my article "Why Presbyterians Do Not Believe that Baptism Saves Souls or Remits Sins," *Reformed Perspectives Magazine*, Volume 12, Number 25. https://goo.gl/U4wQQ1.

[13] WCF 28:1; Baptism is practiced differently in some churches, but its overall meaning and purpose is similar. Presbyterians differ from baptists in at least two ways: 1) Presbyterians baptize by pouring water, like taking a shower, while baptists immerse, like taking a bath. 2) Presbyterians baptize professing Christians *and their children*, while baptists only baptize professing Christians. This does not mean that Presbyterians believe baptism saves children. Once again, see my "Why Presbyterians Do Not Believe Baptism Regenerates Souls or Remits Sins."

[14] The church only baptizes and receives into its number those who profess faith in and obedience unto Christ. As I said in the previous note, presbyterians also baptize their children, believing admission to the church is a family affair. This is different from baptists, who do not baptize the children of professing believers. They wait until after children have made their own profession of faith. Once again, neither baptists nor presbyterians believe baptism saves anyone, and both have long-standing, well-developed, biblically grounded reasons for baptizing as they do.

[15] This is different from how the church used to look at the scope of elder authority. There have been unfortunate times when the church has been too tightly connected to the state and exercised the state's authority to force obedience. During the colonization of the New World, people had more freedom, but still the lines were blurred under the parish system. Over time we have come to realize that the separation of church and state is a good thing, and that church and state should exercise their authority separately. Regardless, the church does not exercise the

"power of the sword," (Romans 13) which at least means that the church cannot force obedience.

[16] Presbyterians would add "and their children" here. Presbyterian beliefs concerning the role of children in church membership are different from baptistic churches. Until children confirm their own faith in Christ, they are under the umbrella of their parents with regard to membership.

[17] The historical mainline denominations were at one time the largest denominations in America: Christian (Disciples of Christ), Reformed Church in America, United Church of Christ (Congregationalist), the Episcopal Church, Presbyterian Church (USA), United Methodist Church, Evangelical Lutheran Church, American Baptist Churches, and others. Although there are some exceptional congregations, the official teaching of these denominations is theologically and socially liberal. Their membership has declined by millions since their heyday.

[18] Some churches have less control because their denominations frequently assign ministers to them, among them are Episcopal, Lutheran, and Methodist churches.

[19] I know of specific examples where presbyterian courts have still failed. This often occurs when process and procedure is used to silence people or allow them to be silenced, which violates the spirit of process and procedure. One change I would make to the presbyterian system would be to require courts to assign complainants an ombudsman or advocate—someone with knowledge of the system, with standing in the courts, and commissioned to advise, represent, and pursue the complainant's interests.

[20] Communion signifies more than what we will discuss here. For example, it causes us to remember Christ's substitutionary sacrifice, signifies his spiritual presence, and proclaims the gospel until he comes again.

[21] This distinction is generally presbyterian. Children of believers are baptized into the visible church as non-communing members, which means they cannot yet participate in communion. Once a church has confirmed that they possess their own faith in Christ, they will be admitted to communing membership.

[22] However, maybe it is a church plant—a new church that someone is trying to start. If that is the case, look at what the organizers are trying to accomplish, compare their goals to what the church is supposed to be, and then, if it appears biblical, consider keeping it on your list.

[23] Be aware, however, that presbyterians who try to join baptist churches are usually required to be rebaptized before being accepted. Presbyterians, on the other hand, will receive any valid baptism from any other denomination. Before presbyterians submit to rebaptism, they should see my "Why Presbyterians Only Baptize Once" in *Reformed Perspectives Magazine*, Volume 12, Number 24. https://goo.gl/NCTrUx.

[24] http://www.capitolhillbaptist.org/about-us/what-we-believe/church-covenant/

[25] Protestantism is that part of the church that is not Roman Catholic or Eastern Orthodox. During the Reformation in the 1500's, Christians began protesting the

teachings of the Roman Catholic Church. Out of this were born the protestant denominations: Lutherans, Anglicans, Presbyterians, Baptists, Methodists, etc.

[26] Robert Peterson in *Why We Belong: Evangelical Unity and Denominational Diversity* (Wheaton: Crossway, 2013), 63.

[27] Erickson, *Christian Theology*, 1033.

[28] The issue of baptism provides an example of how this "Golden Rule" actually unifies the church. As a matter of conviction, Baptists only baptize believers by immersion. Presbyterians, by their conviction, baptize the children of believers by affusion (sprinkling). Neither is willing to give up this conviction because both strongly believe it to be based upon God's Word. Furthermore, if they were to unite, Baptists would require Presbyterians to be rebaptized because they do not accept the validity of Presbyterian baptism. Presbyterians on the other hand have a strong conviction against rebaptism. These mutually exclusive convictions (among others) prevent the denominations from uniting. The existence of separate denominations permits each to honor their own convictions, to exist at relative peace within the larger body, and to sometimes develop relationships and cooperative partnerships across denominational boundaries without expecting the other to compromise sincerely held convictions.

www.ingramcontent.com/pod-product-compliance
Lightning Source LLC
Chambersburg PA
CBHW071515040426
42444CB00008B/1653